20.63
SWEAT SHIRTS
SOCCER

TOMMY WALKER

with Marcus Brotherton

BREAK THROUGH

Regal

From Gospel Light
Ventura, California, U.S.A.

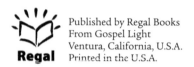

Published by Regal Books
From Gospel Light
Ventura, California, U.S.A.
Printed in the U.S.A.

Regal Books is a ministry of Gospel Light, a Christian publisher dedicated to serving the local church. We believe God's vision for Gospel Light is to provide church leaders with biblical, user-friendly materials that will help them evangelize, disciple and minister to children, youth and families.

It is our prayer that this Regal book will help you discover biblical truth for your own life and help you meet the needs of others. May God richly bless you.

For a free catalog of resources from Regal Books/Gospel Light, please call your Christian supplier or contact us at 1-800-4-GOSPEL or www.regalbooks.com.

Library of Congress Cataloging-in-Publication Data
Walker, Tommy.
  Breakthrough / Tommy Walker with Marcus Brotherton.
     p. cm.
  ISBN 0-8307-3914-9 (hard cover)
  1. Christian life. I. Brotherton, Marcus. II. Title.
  BV4501.3.W354 2006
  248.4—dc22   2005035298

1   2   3   4   5   6   7   8   9   10   /   10   09   08   07   06

Rights for publishing this book in other languages are contracted by Gospel Light Worldwide, the international nonprofit ministry of Gospel Light. For additional information, visit www.gospellightworldwide.org; write to Gospel Light Worldwide, P.O. Box 3875, Ventura, CA 93006; or send an e-mail to info@gospellightworldwide.org.

CONTENTS

ACKNOWLEDGMENTS

I want to thank my brother Dale Walker. Dale, you have been one of my spiritual heroes in this life and have certainly modeled what a breakthrough Christian looks like. The stories and words that are yours in this book came from your life with God and had a huge impact on what this book became. Thanks for all the time and inspiration you brought to this project!

To Marcus Brotherton. This book was a team effort, and you were definitely the star player. What a gifted man you are! I celebrate God's writing gift in you and pray that this book will be a small part of the Lord broadening your ministry influence in the world. To my new friend, I say thank you!

To my editor, Deena Davis. If there weren't people like you who know every rule of spelling and grammar there is, there certainly wouldn't be people like me writing books like this! Thanks for all your hard work and for giving so much more than just the correct way to say something. You put your heart and soul into this project, and your own love for God is certainly on these pages as well. Thank you!

To Kim Bangs, for coming up with the original idea for this book. To Bill Greig III, and to the entire Gospel Light staff, for believing in me.

To my other brothers, Jerry and Steve, and to my mom—for the breakthrough thoughts you gave me.

And most important, to my Lord and Savior, Jesus Christ.

It always amazes me how God takes our seemingly small and insignificant choices and uses them in such significant ways. I made a choice to pray while driving in my truck one day, and a song was born. And now I am writing thank-yous for this book because of that song. God is truly the rewarder of those who diligently seek Him! I feel so privileged and blessed to be able to share the many ways that God has broken through in my life; and I am overwhelmed to think that He is willing to bring His life-altering, breakthrough power to others through the message of these pages. For all of this, I say, "THANK YOU, God," for letting me be on Your team in this life, for letting me play not just on the bench but in the game, and for letting me wear Your colors and bear Your name as a Christian! The fact that You would allow me to play the smallest role in Your work on Earth is a reminder to me—and I hope to everyone reading—that You're a God who chooses the unlikely ones to score the touchdown. O God, forever I will thank You!

This book was once a song . . .

BREAK THROUGH

Break through, break through all my doubts
Break through, break through all my fears
Break through that I may worship You.
Break through, break through all my pain
Break through all my guilt and my shame
Break through like only You can do.

You are brighter than my darkest night
Stronger than my toughest fight
Just one touch from You my King, my Friend
And I'll never be the same again.[1]

Note

1. Tommy Walker, "Break Through," © 2005.

ARE YOU READY FOR A BREAKTHROUGH?

> The key to living a
> Breakthrough Life is to know
> the Breakthrough God!

I have a passionate hope. I hope that something you read in these pages will somehow strike a resonating chord in your soul and make you yearn to know the God of the breakthrough more deeply and follow Him more closely. The older I get, the more plainly I see this truth: All that we are and ever hope to be rides on one thing—*our relationship with Him.*

I know that when I'm breaking through the obstacles that are a fact of life, and I find my way to Him, everything else just falls into place. There's a very good reason for this cause-and-effect relationship: We were made by God with a need to know Him, to believe in Him and to worship and serve Him.

If we don't learn to go deep with God, we will try to fight life's battles without Him and will find only a shallow, meaningless existence. No one wants that kind of life. So come with me on a journey. It won't take long. Come with me to a place where the sky opens up and the God who created us breaks through into our darkened and discouraged hearts to give us the Light of the World—Jesus Christ Himself!

More than anything, this book is about worship. There's something about a surrendered heart of worship that positions us like nothing else for a life-altering God encounter—for that breakthrough moment with Him! It is about letting those encounters with Him redraw the lines of our potential. Jesus has come to set us free—familiar words that we should never take for granted. He is the God of the breakthrough! When He breaks through, we are connected with the Source of all blessing.

When breakthrough occurs, we may not have all the answers and we may not understand why or how we've arrived at the place where we need breakthrough so desperately, but we will have a Presence.

It's the presence of Jesus. And because of Him, we have a launching pad for the life we so desperately long for. Not only do we find endurance and strength, but we also find the ability to be overcomers and "blessers"—people who bless others because we've been blessed.

God alone is the One Thing you and I must seek. He alone is the object of our worship. I encourage you—I implore you not to wait. Give Him your pain. Give Him your questions, your doubts, your fears, your will, your life—and be His worshiper. Then get ready for a breakthrough!

Tommy Walker
Eagle Rock, California
January 2006

CHAPTER 1

INTO HIS PRESENCE

> [He] is able to do immeasurably
> more than all we ask or imagine,
> according to His power that
> is within us.
>
> EPHESIANS 3:20

About a year ago, I was sitting in church worshiping God. Or so it looked. It was a morning when I wasn't up front leading, so I was enjoying a rare time of sitting next to my wife and two oldest kids (my two youngest kids were at children's church). But truthfully, I wasn't actually worshiping. I was just singing—politely keeping my head in the game.

I wouldn't call what I was doing "faking"—not exactly. It was more a hesitancy. I knew there could be more to the morning than what I was willing to allow. But I didn't want to let God disturb me. I was tired. *I don't have the time or energy to go deep with God right now,* I thought as I sang. *I simply don't want to go there.*

I imagine it has happened to all of us—this settling for something less. We take one step toward Him and then two steps back. We temporarily forget that what we truly want is Him. Who is this God who beckons us closer, invites us to know Him, to experience Him—to taste and see that He is good? This is the same God whom the prophet Isaiah saw, as recorded in the sixth chapter of the book of Isaiah. He saw God seated on a throne, high and exalted, with the train of His robe filling the Temple. Angels covered their faces in this God's presence and called to one another: *Holy, holy, holy is the LORD Almighty.*

I thought about such an image, sitting in church that morning. I thought about a God who prompts that type of awed reaction when a person encounters Him. Truly, I know that God is better than anything I can imagine—anything that I love on Earth—amazing sunsets, the Pacific Ocean, the smell of barbecued steak as it drifts through my neighborhood, the smile of my wife, Robin, as she greets me when I come home from work. God is greater still. *Why wouldn't I want this?* I thought. *Why wouldn't I want to actually worship Him with all my heart, soul, mind and strength?*

I could sense God moving me. "Meet Me here," God seemed to whisper. "Don't just attend church this morning because you want to be a good husband or a good dad. Don't just settle for singing. Worship in spirit and truth. Connect with Me entirely. Believe in Me fully. Know Me more closely than you have before." There was a deepness to the Voice—not a pressure, but an urgency—an invitation to an incredible celebration that I couldn't miss.

Is this not what we long for in a life of faith? Do we not want to truly experience more of God?

And so I stopped—I stopped resisting, and I yielded. I *let*.

In an act of surrender, I raised my voice and my hands and opened my heart to the King of kings. I was not just singing anymore. The same God who spreads out the sky over empty space, who marks out the horizon, who churns up the sea so that its waters roar—this God met me that morning. I worshiped.

It was a breakthrough.

God was so near to me that morning that He came crashing through time and space and touched the deepest part of my heart. It's not that this was a life-altering experience; in fact, on the outside it probably didn't look like much. But it is in these seemingly insignificant moments that God wants to—in an ongoing way—break through in our lives. No, I didn't hear Him audibly. No fire from heaven singed my clothes. It was more like that indescribable sense that He was there. The God of heaven was with me. Later, I sensed the Lord confirm to me promises that I had been reading in His Word:

- Draw near to God, and He will draw near to you (see Jas. 4:7).
- He is the rewarder of those who diligently seek Him (see Heb. 11:6).
- Though we have not seen Him, we love Him; and even though we do not see Him now, we believe in Him and are filled with an inexpressible and glorious joy (see 1 Pet. 1:8).

The last promise in particular was the place I had come to. I was filled with an inexpressible and glorious joy! For the rest of the day I walked around with a smile in my heart. I couldn't explain it, but I felt empowered with a new sense of His presence in my life.

LEARNING HOW TO LET

This book was written to help you understand how to receive a breakthrough from God—or I should say, receive a breakthrough *to* God. Maybe you're a Christian who years ago mumbled The Sinner's Prayer but haven't moved an inch deeper in your walk with Christ since then. Your invitation is to learn how to take hold of the Holy Spirit's power that awaits you.

Perhaps you know the Lord in a personal way, but it has been decades since you've had any sort of change in your spiritual walk. Your invitation is to allow God to do His daily work in your life. Maybe you simply want more—more faith, more passion, more grace, more perseverance, more obedience, more forgiveness. You're stuck in some kind of rut that prevents these things, but you don't know how to move from where you're at to where you want to be.

God wants you to break through. A breakthrough comes when we advance through an obstacle or opposition. Often it comes quickly and suddenly; but sometimes it comes slowly and over time. A breakthrough means that we push through and move past whatever oppressive barrier is in front of us.

Something is holding us down, holding us back, holding us under—and the barrier can be so intense that it can stop our life. Or it may be so habitual that it just keeps entangling us. I don't know anyone stuck in a rut who doesn't, deep down, long for a breakthrough. There is hope in a breakthrough—we want to experience God in a way that is true and deep. We want to be free. We don't want to stay the same.

What holds us back? What keeps us stuck? I call these hindrances "breakthrough blockers." Blockers are anything that prevents us from receiving a touch of the resurrected, ever-present Jesus. He is always there, waiting, at hand. He wants to meet us in powerful ways. He invites us into new worlds of reality and possibility—the present heavenly reality of the kingdom of God. But these blockers prevent breakthrough.

Have you ever experienced anything like this?

- *Doubt.* You would like to believe in a God who is good and who cares for you—but something tragic has just happened in your life. How can God be good and have allowed that tragedy to happen? You just can't believe Him.
- *Fear.* You know there's a better way to live. But to get there involves risk. You have to

change something in your life; and although your life is painful right now, at least it's familiar. Your patterns are like an old shoe— a bit broken down, with a hole in the sole— but comfortable. Holding on to something, even if it's harmful, seems easier than letting go, even when it's to hold on to something much better.

· *Pain.* Sometimes pain can be so intense that it just makes us want to close up shop and go home. Sometimes pain can drift along in our lives for years, only rising to the surface in moments of stress or tiredness. But usually our cry is the same: *God, why aren't You taking away my pain?*

· *Guilt.* The places we've been, the things we've done. How could God love us when He knows about our past? We would truly come to Him—truly walk with the Lord—but there's just so much junk cluttering the way. How can we truly let go and walk in freedom?

There are more breakthrough blockers: hurriedness, disobedience, laziness, bitterness, jealousy, wrong concepts of God, comparison with others; the list is virtually endless. God doesn't call us to stay focused on our blockers; He calls us to focus on Him. The enemy has come to steal, kill and destroy, but Christ has come so that we can have life, and have it to the full (see John 10:10). Still, the blockers are real, and they can plague our life like nothing else. That's what we'll take a look at in this book. In the chapters ahead we're going to look at some of the most common blockers and how to position ourselves before God for that one touch from Him that will move us to a breakthrough.

A story is told of General Jonathan Wainright, a prisoner of war who suffered horribly in the enemy prison camps of World War II. He was tortured, oppressed and robbed of any freedom he had. But the day of emancipation came. News broke that the Japanese had surrendered. The war was over, and U.S. forces were now actually governing the very prison camp where General Wainright had been held prisoner. In fact, General Wainright was now in command there—in this same place where he had been forced to yield his life to slavery.

For a few days the news seemed too good to be true. Though the tables were turned and the enemy officers who had tortured him were actually prison-

ers now, some of them still tried to intimidate and
threaten General Wainright. For several days he hesitated. It was so difficult for him to let go of the
mind-set of his past.

What saved him was this: The General secured a
copy of the emancipation papers and read carefully
what was written. It was true; he was no longer a
prisoner. Then he went to the enemy officers, declaring that they were absolutely defeated and had no
authority or power anymore. They were not in
charge anymore. General Wainright broke through
and took command of the camp. He was victorious
from that moment onward.

Breakthroughs can be like that. Our blockers
can seem overwhelming. What we're going through
can feel too strong, too tough, too dark. The voice of
the enemy can be heard every day if we let it speak
(*God doesn't care about you; who do you think you are anyway?*).

But let God remind us of who we are in Christ.
Blockers such as fear, doubt, inadequacy and guilt
will give way as we stand in the truths of God's
Word. Barriers will come down as we become con-
vinced of our new identity. We are no longer slaves.
We are free!

GOING TO HIM FIRST

In the pages ahead, I want to introduce you to something so wonderful and powerful that when it comes into your life, you'll never be the same again. These are breakthrough moments when hope and opportunity meet in such a way that they change the landscape of time and create realities only dreamed of before.

That's what a breakthrough can be like.

Think of the fall of the Berlin Wall and the Iron Curtain of communism. Suddenly people's lives were changed from the fear of oppression to the possibility of freedom. What a breakthrough!

Think of Dr. Salk and the discovery of a vaccine that would eradicate the horrors of polio, a disease that ruined tens of thousands of people's lives, even crippling the body of President Franklin Roosevelt. What a breakthrough!

Think of a rocket ship breaking through Earth's atmosphere, heading for the moon. Astronauts land on a place and walk where no man has ever walked before. What a breakthrough!

All of these things were once called impossible. All of these things began with a dream and a vision that brought people to a point of opportunity. Once that opportunity was seized and commitment was applied to the goal, a breakthrough occurred. The same way these breakthroughs have come to Earth, breakthroughs can come into our lives in the spiritual realm. Impossible achievements can be accomplished, hurts and heartbreaks can be healed, barriers to great potential and global-sized dreams can be overcome.

But I want to be careful here, because the answer isn't just to have more faith, to pray more, to crank up more courage or to just buck up. The answer is to draw close to the person of God Himself. That is where our starting point lies; it's also where our ending point lies. We must seek the face of the Almighty. The power and the strength to live a God-honoring life are found in the presence and joy of the Lord, not in striving or working. He is our first step. Seek first the kingdom of God and all these things shall be added to you (see Matt. 6:33). The key to breakthrough is that we don't seek *things* first; we seek *Him*. Within the personhood of Christ we find breakthrough, because He's the breakthrough God!

God is not a reluctant God waiting to be awakened. He is a passionate God who has from eternity planned to intervene in the very circumstances we go through. God has every solution to our problems, even before those problems exist. He planned for a Savior before there were sinners. The touch of the resurrected, ever-present Jesus is available, waiting and at hand if we will only ask for it. That touch is there, waiting, at the end of our broken dreams, our difficult losses, fears and failures.

I want to describe some of the times that I have found breakthrough in Christ, and I want to invite you, in and through Jesus Christ, to enter into this new world of possibility. When you have an unblocked, ongoing relationship with Him, you will discover all the fringe benefits of being with Him. Relationship with God brings an entirely new world of possibilities to our lives.

AND I SANG

There's more to the story of the day I was sitting in church and experienced a breakthrough. It's what happened in my life to bring me to that place. I've already mentioned that I was tired that day—but it wasn't just physical tiredness; it was the type of deep soul tiredness that comes when you sorrow. The entire year preceding that day had been a year of blows, not to me necessarily, but to people I loved and cared about. I was feeling an exhaustion that comes when people close to you have been through the wringer.

The first blow came to my cousin, Kim. She's my age, with two young boys. When we were kids, she and I went to kindergarten together. There's this picture of us back then—my hair is all slicked back; she looks like an all-American dark-haired cutie. She grew up to be a beauty queen, and when she was diagnosed with cancer, the disease ravaged her body in horrible ways. A week before she died, a powerful prayer meeting was held. I come from a strong, praying Christian family, and I was told they had really pressed in to God that day. Everyone got their hopes up, including me.

I sang at the funeral.

The second blow came to Ed Monroe, a friend of mine at church. Ed was a construction worker. He loved the Lord and took great pride in his work. He widened my driveway once and was always popping by my office, wanting to buy me lunch. He had always been in good health; but one day, at about age 50, he got sick very suddenly. When I visited him at home on his deathbed, I remember him saying, "Oh Tommy, it's such a beautiful day. The Lord is so good." He was gasping for air, talking slowly, smiling in spite of the labored sound of his cancer-filled lungs.

I sang at the funeral.

The third blow came to a family in our church with two teenage kids. The husband, Conrad Pickard, sings in the choir I lead. I've known them for about 12 years. One day, the mom got a headache, very bad this time; she had been getting dizzy spells for a while, but then she knew something was wrong. I visited her in the hospital and prayed for her. Every summer the family would camp on the same California beach. When she died, her family had her body cremated. I went with them and stood with the teenage kids on the shore while their father waded into the water at sunset. He let his wife's ashes slowly slip away on the outgoing tide from the beach they all loved.

I sang at the funeral.

The fourth blow came to Aria, the 11-year-old daughter of friends of mine, Jeff and Belinda Lams. Jeff is a keyboard session player here in town. He's been in bands that have led worship at Franklin Graham crusades, so a lot of people know him and were following this situation. Aria had battled leukemia since she was three. Can you imagine your baby girl going through this? She fought like a soldier, getting better, getting worse, for seven years. Over time, an e-mail chain of prayer supporters grew into the hundreds. I would imagine that even Billy Graham prayed for Aria, but God had other plans. Aria died with her family at her side that day. Her battle was finally over.

I sang at the funeral.

After four funerals in a year, my heart was crying to the Lord: *God, where are You? God, why? God, what possible reason could You have for allowing all this?!* No, none of these blows happened to me, but I felt them all. This was my God who was in control of these situations. All of them. Sometimes God allows such crazy events to take place; we'll just never know why. That whole year had been one of those years. Sitting in church, I was feeling a sense of weight—a cloud of sorrow. There was an accumulation of events I couldn't grasp with my brain, and my spirit felt like curling into a ball and lying on the floor. *God, how can I worship You through this—all of this?*

The answer?

I had to *let.*

My brain does not comprehend the mind of Christ. "How faint the whisper we hear of him! Who then can understand the thunder of his power?"

(Job 26:14). Only when God breaks through can my spirit leap for joy. I don't check my brains at the door, but there's a knowledge that comes and supersedes what I can grasp—it's the knowledge of the Holy. Only with this knowledge can we declare with confidence, "The LORD gave and the LORD has taken away; may the name of the LORD be praised" (Job 1:21).

This was the breakthrough I received that morning. I didn't have all the answers. These four people whom I cared about had died and did not come back to life again. But I returned to that secret place with the Lord again. There I could see that God was greater than any problem. In His presence I could face life by faith and not by sight. It was the breakthrough that allowed me to say, even when all was not well with my circumstances, that all was well with my soul.

This is the breakthrough God invites us to—a breakthrough to Him.

BRIGHTER THAN OUR DARKEST NIGHTS

In what area of your life do you need a breakthrough? Perhaps it's a small area; perhaps it's big. Our hope is this: If we have just one touch from the Lord, we will never be the same again. A breakthrough happens when the strength of God suddenly encounters and overwhelms our weaknesses. It's when the provision of God suddenly encompasses our lack. It's when the darkness of confusion is enveloped in the divine wisdom of God.

When I think of a God who is no stranger to breakthroughs, I think of John 1:5, where it describes the light shining in the darkness, and the darkness could not overcome it. My mom likes to say that darkness can never hide light; darkness only magnifies light. Darkness is the canvass that brings out the beauty and the glory of God's gracious intervention. When it gets dark in a theater, it's time for the story to begin.

What is your story—the one that is waiting to begin? This book is an invitation to that story, an opportunity to encounter something incredible, good and true: the Something that overcomes the night, that lifts you from the miry clay, that offers you a glimpse of a miraculous life.

Break through to this new life. Break through into the presence of the Almighty. He's closer than you think!

PRAYER

Oh, Lord, You said that if I would draw near to
You, You would draw near to me. In the midst of
my questions and sadness, I run to You. I don't
feel like I even know how to do this, but I begin
by simply declaring that You are good; You are
worthy; You are God! I choose to worship You;
and as I do, I pray that—by your faithful, unmer-
ited, amazing grace—You will break through and
draw near to me now. Amen.

BREAK THROUGH DOUBTS

> See to it . . . that none of you
> has a sinful, unbelieving heart that
> turns away from the living God.
>
> HEBREWS 3:12

The choices we make can help bring a breakthrough.
One of the greatest choices we can make is to believe
that God is who He says He is. Having faith is essen-
tial. We can't break through to God if we don't
believe in Him. Having faith is when we take God at
His word—no matter what our circumstances—and
choose to believe that He is real, that He answers
prayers, that He is good and that He loves us—always.

Having faith is seldom easy. Sometimes faith
looks like a quiet step forward. Sometimes it looks

like a huge leap. To whatever extent God stretches and increases our faith, His invitation to us is always to believe that He cares about us and loves us.

WHEN DOUBT SHUTS US DOWN

I believe that battle number one in our spiritual lives is the battle for our faith. Faith is the key that opens the door to our salvation. Faith is also necessary in our everyday lives until that great day when we see Him face to face and our faith becomes sight. This life-journey we're on brings us many opportunities to decide who and what we're going to believe in and on what foundation we're going to stake our lives. Tough, unexplainable circumstances continually urge us to throw away our ability and desire to have faith in an invisible God.

To clarify, when I talk about doubt being a problem, I'm not talking about the healthy kind of questioning that spurs us to arrive at truth. A lot of false belief systems require a blind allegiance to whatever they're offering—just chuck your brains and believe. But Jesus Christ isn't like that. Our faith is rooted in evidence and truth, and there are many exemplary God-fearing apologists, archaeologists, professors and scholars who spend their lives researching and proving facts about the existence of God, the historic authenticity of

Jesus, the textual reliability of the Scriptures, and the irrefutable circumstances surrounding the resurrection of Christ. True faith doesn't circumvent intelligence.

The type of doubt that's a problem is the doubt that shuts us down. This doubt is when we wonder if God truly makes a difference in our lives. This doubt makes us question God's goodness—does He really intervene and hear our prayers? Is God trustworthy? Does He actually care for us? Is He who He says He is?

This is the type of doubt that makes us say things like:

- Here I am, 35 and single. I always thought I'd be married by now. I love the Lord, but why hasn't He blessed me in this way? Maybe God doesn't really care about me.
- I know the Lord wants me to volunteer at church in a new way and be a greater influence for Him. But what if I fail? Can God really take me through the challenges I know I'm going to encounter in this new role?
- I've tried for so long to kick this one habit, but nothing seems to work. Maybe I'm too far gone. Is God really big enough to bring about a lasting change in my life?

- Why did this hurricane that I'm seeing on the news ravage so many lives? God could have stopped it, but He didn't. Why? When I see stuff like this it makes me doubt His existence. Are You real, God? Are You truly good?

Right now my dad is 79. Before he retired, he was a pastor of a large church and a man of great vision and leadership ability. A few years back he began having constant irrational thoughts—just little uncertainties at first—*Are you sure you locked the front door?*—but the questions grew louder. What he heard began to affect others.

"Honey," he would say to my mom, "did I lock the house?"

"Yes, Honey, you did."

"But are you sure? Are you positive? Because I really don't think I did."

"Yes, Honey, I'm sure."

"We need to go home—I don't believe you. The front door is unlocked. We've got to go home right now!"

Today, Dad's brain doesn't always function like it used to. His doubts sometimes overtake him. A while ago, he was diagnosed with Alzheimer's—and in some ways that takes the pressure off all who interact with him. Dad lives daily as an extreme example of a man entrapped by faulty perceptions—through no fault of his own, we know now.

But still it's hard. Dad has days when he questions everything. I'm so proud of him though. Every day he makes a conscious choice to keep reading his Bible and pray. He once told my mom that the most precious gift God had given him was the ability to choose faith. He's choosing to be a man of faith, fighting his doubts and this disease to the end. Through it all, my dad is courageously showing me how to end well and choose faith, even when faith isn't the easiest choice!

Doubt can be like spiritual Alzheimer's. Doubt makes us forget what we know to be true. Doubt attacks us, driving us under. It makes us stay walking in a rut. Doubt is a breakthrough blocker.

But there is hope.

STEPPING BEYOND THE POSSIBLE

Besides the Psalms, I think that the book of Hebrews is my favorite book in the Bible, because it encourages us in our faith. Hebrews reminds us that if we don't believe and have faith, we will stray from God and not receive His promises and blessings. When we were created in the image of God, He created us with an ability to believe what is not seen. Hebrews 12:1-2 says that He is the author and creator of our faith.

Breakthrough comes when we choose the path of believing. When we're in the midst of suffering and pain, the light of hope can break through by faith, filling us with the strength to persevere. Job is a great example of this kind of faith. He loses everything—his children, family members, house, wealth. His health is also devastated with a horrible skin disease. Job is in so much inner turmoil and physical pain that he takes a broken piece of pottery and scrapes his body, just trying to get some relief from his affliction. Despite everything, he doesn't curse God. He knows that he has a choice. He declares, "Though he slay me, yet will I hope in Him" (Job 13:15). At one of his lowest points, Job cries out, "I know that my Redeemer lives, and that in the end he will stand upon the earth. And after my skin has been destroyed, yet in my flesh I will see God" (19:25-26). Job had chosen not to become bitter. He worshiped. He surrendered his doubt of God's goodness, and believed.

Virtually all of us, when faced with challenging circumstances, jump to conclusions. If we live by doubt, we will jump to negative conclusions. If we live by faith, we will jump to victory conclusions. We will assume that God's power, provision, protection and promises are enough.

But faith, more than simply having a positive attitude, is a decision to yield our hearts in complete alignment with God's will. In 2 Chronicles 20, we find an amazing example of the kind of faith that brings breakthrough in an impossible situation. King Jehoshaphat wakes up one day to find his country surrounded by armies a hundred times greater than his own. It's too late to negotiate, to come up with an escape. He and his people are totally hemmed in.

In distress, Jehoshaphat chooses to turn his focus and attention from the catastrophic circumstances to the amazing greatness of God. He utterly surrenders to the Lord: "We do not know what to do, but our eyes are upon you" (v. 13). (Isn't that a great prayer to remember in whatever challenging circumstances we face?) In his surrender, Jehoshaphat humbles his heart and aligns himself with God's will—whatever God's will may be.

Here we see a tremendous example of breakthrough. When we position ourselves before the Lord in a place of complete surrender and obedience during a time of crisis, God is able to show His character to us in ways we could never imagine. In Jehoshaphat's situation, the Lord chooses to speak through a prophet: "You will not have to fight this battle. Take up your positions; stand firm and see the deliverance the LORD will give you. . . . Go out and face them tomorrow and the LORD will be with you" (v. 17).

Having relinquished control of the situation to God, Jehoshaphat appoints a choir to sing to the Lord for the splendor of His holiness. Instead of fighting the battle, Jehoshaphat chooses to worship—isn't that incredible? As the rest of the story goes, after the Israelites begin to sing and praise, the Lord stirs up the enemy to fight each other. All that is left behind by the time Jehoshaphat reaches the battlefield is the wealth of the enemies' possessions to take back home.

When we surrender our abilities, as strong or as weak as they might be, and we choose to worship Him, God will fight our battles for us!

Faith always involves an action. It always involves a risk that often seems weird to the natural mind. Jesus challenged Peter in the midst of a storm to walk on water. Jesus told a man with a withered hand to stretch it out—and it was healed. God puts the seed of faith in our hearts in the midst of a crisis, but then He waits for us to go and sow that seed, take action and step beyond the possible. At that point, Christ steps in and moves. The Bible tells of a woman who had been bleeding for 12 years—she wasn't healed until she reached out, pushed through a crowd and touched the hem of Jesus' garment. That's our task as well: to position ourselves, to reach out and touch the hem of the Person of Christ.

Faith involves not only seeing the promises of God, but it also "involves moving from a point of pleading to a point of praising."[1] Faith is when we stop telling God how big our mountain is and start telling our mountain how big our God is. I wish I could shout from the rooftop to every believer: *God will fight our battles for us!* He is waiting to bring glory to His name as we learn to stand back and let Him move and work in our lives.

Determination is part of the solution. Faith comes when we make a series of what looks like small decisions: Yes, I'm going to be a man or woman of faith; yes, I'm going to be a believer and not a doubter; yes, I will follow Christ wholeheartedly no matter what my circumstances.

But to be clear, faith is not obtained *by* our determination. We obtain faith by hearing God's Word, by ingesting it into our hearts and by responding to Him in worship. We perfect our faith by fixing our eyes on Him—on His strength and beauty. That's where our joy and strength come from.

WHEN THE "NEXT-DAY VOICE" SPEAKS

What practical step do we need to take when we find ourselves doubting God? I may just choose to end every chapter the same way in this book—because the solution doesn't change, no matter what our break-through blocker is. The solution is *worship*. When we see the Lord for who He is, we take our gaze from ourselves and look on Him. In His presence we find the one thing we need.

I saw a powerful example of this at the funeral for Scott Bauer, senior pastor of The Church On The Way, in Van Nuys, California. Jack Hayford, his predecessor, had groomed Scott for years to assume the role, and Scott had done really well in that role. He preached the Word of God, led his congregation to greater depths of spiritual maturity, and reached out to his community with the love of Christ. People loved Pastor Scott.

At the end of a service, he slumped over suddenly from a brain aneurysm. He lived for only a few days and then went to be with the Lord. He was only 49. I'll never forget being at his funeral. There were thousands of people in attendance, grieving the pastor they loved so dearly. At the end of the service, everyone was singing Matt and Beth Redman's song "Blessed Be Your Name" and kept singing passionately the last lines of the song: "You give and take away, You give and take away, my heart will choose to say, blessed be Your name!"[2] It was one of the most extreme experiences of my life. The death of Pastor Scott Bauer didn't make sense. But any doubts we might have had of the purposes, plans and goodness of God were being pushed back as we worshiped. My brain wasn't getting it all, but my spirit was leaping for joy.

Only by faith can we sing words like those in "Blessed Be Your Name."

Faith doesn't stop there. Faith is needed the next day and the next day and the day after that. Faith answers all the "next-day voices"—the lies that tell us, *Well, that wasn't anything. What's wrong with you anyway? That was just a bunch of foolish people in there singing that song.*

In those instances, we have to make a choice. No! I have to believe that the experience of singing at Scott Bauer's funeral was of the Lord. I have to open my Bible and read His promises. I have to open my mouth and verbally bless the Lord. *Lord, You are great. Lord, You are good. Lord, blessed be Your name.* Satan is a liar and a thief, and he wants to steal away those precious times of breakthrough that God gives us, those most meaningful moments. It's the next day when the Devil says, "That wasn't anything; that was just you."

We must treasure the times that the Lord gives us, those times when He touches us in incredible ways. By faith, no one can take those moments away from us. *Break through . . . break through all my doubts, Lord Jesus. I will worship You in the midst of the struggle. I will choose to honor you with a heart of faith this day.*

PRAYER

Lord, I believe You are greater and deeper than these doubts that haunt me. You created me for faith. From the beginning of time, everything about me was designed to operate out of a context of trusting and believing in You. Now, oh Holy Spirit, as I declare my faith in You, come pierce through my darkness. Come and break through my doubts like only the One who is the creator of my faith can do. Amen.

Notes

1. Wayne Myers with Mary Dunham Faulkner, *Living Beyond the Possible* (McLean, VA: Evangeline Press, 2003), n.p.

2. Matt and Beth Redman, "Blessed Be Your Name," © 2002 Thankyou Music. Administered by worshiptogether.com songs. Exclusive U.K. and Europe, administered by Kingsway Music: tym@kingsway.co.uk.

CHAPTER 3

BREAK THROUGH FEAR

> For God did not give us a spirit
> of fear, but a spirit of power,
> of love, and of a sound mind.
>
> TIMOTHY 1:7

When I was growing up, I stayed in my room a lot, playing guitar. It's what shy people do—stay inside. It always feels safer there. After I graduated from high school in 1979, I went to Bible college for two years in Dallas. Then for several months I just sort of drifted.

For a while I stayed in Dallas, working for a moving company while playing in a band. I made good cash from lugging around office equipment in downtown Dallas—enough from one weekend so that I wouldn't have to work the rest of the month. I played guitar for a Christian singer, too, and we went to Africa on a mission trip that year.

Something significant happened on that trip. On the way back home, we stopped in London, where the seeds of a lifelong vision were planted in me. I saw a group of Christian young people in a park who were singing so that anyone passing by could listen. I remember thinking, *If I could worship God so freely in front of nonbelievers, and if I did it with excellence, that kind of worship could be an incredible tool to bring people to Christ.* Their public worship was just so raw, so unencumbered—so *out there*. I wanted to do something like that too. And I wanted to make sure that I did it to the best of my ability. I began to think about going to music school to hone my skills. I didn't yet know how or where that would happen; I just began to feel this passion for something more than I was doing.

It took years to realize my dream. I moved back to El Paso, Texas, where I grew up. I got a job in a factory, stacking sticks from a conveyor belt all day long. My job was to crate them up. That was my whole life. I would look at my watch all the time. When it felt like four hours had gone by, only four minutes had passed. I finally quit the factory and got another job loading freight on a dock.

For a time, I did jingles for local radio and TV ads. My favorite was for Ample Duds, a clothing store for plus-size women. Writing jingles was a fun job, but I knew it wasn't my destination. I became aware of my limitations and knew that I needed to go to music school to become a better musician. But first I had to earn the money to go there.

For a while, I lived in Santa Fe, New Mexico, and lived in a barn with a friend who I had met in Dallas, who was a drummer. I delivered pizzas at night. The barn was infected with mice and so cold that the toilet would freeze over in winter months. I managed to save $500, but at the end of that year my transmission froze up, and I spent all my savings on car repairs.

When I had finally saved up enough money, I knew it was time. It was either now or never. I had to step out. God was calling me to lead worship, the type of worship I had seen in that London park, but with skillful creativity. At least that's what I was shooting for. I knew that going to music school in Hollywood was the place to begin that dream. But fear still filled my mind and heart. And my friends were skeptical. "You'll be back before you know it," they said. "Los Angeles is a crazy place. A lot of things can go wrong in California. Nobody leaves El Paso for long."

Truth was, I *was* afraid. There are a lot of good reasons to be afraid of change. But I also knew that if I never took a risk, I would never know what might happen. I wanted to be the best that I could be, and I knew that I had to step out to do that.

At age 26, I jumped. I quit my job, loaded up my '77 El Camino, and headed for Hollywood. Everything I owned fit in or on that old car. A couple hundred miles down the road, a garment bag blew out the back—I lost my best shirt and a bunch of clothes along the desert on Interstate 10. But there was no turning back. It was time to follow God's leading to California.

How would you answer the following questions: What is God's calling for *my* life? Am I on the path I need to be today? If not, why not? What will get me headed in the right direction?

I'm convinced that nothing can keep us from a breakthrough the way that fear can. Fear can prevent us from fulfilling our calling; it can make us want to run and hide. Fear is what keeps us inside where we think we're safe—inside our houses, inside our churches, inside our masks, inside our addictions. The outside is unknown, so why venture there?

Fear makes us want to stay in El Paso, working on a loading dock. (I'm not picking on El Paso or working on a loading dock. It's a perfectly fine place to live and work, but it wasn't the right place for me at that time.)

Perhaps you're not in a horrible situation, but you know you're not where you need to be. You're not where you *could* be if only fear didn't prevent you from moving ahead.

All of us need to continually open our eyes to the Lord's world and ask what that world might look like for us. *God, take us to that place; help us overcome our fears; move us to the place where You want us to be.*

COPERS OR CATALYSTS?

Not only can our fears cripple us, but fears also can actually put us in a position in which we're unable to receive some of the Lord's blessings. We can stake our lives on the fact that we're secure in God's grace and never need to worry that our actions will cause Him to love or care for us less. But some blessings only happen when we respond to Him—when we risk, when we dream, when we step out. Fear prompted the man who received only one talent to dig a hole, hide it in the ground and eventually incur the wrath of his master (see Matt. 25:18). When we give in to our fears, we squander what we've been given.

Fear makes us say things such as:

- There's this dream, this calling, this opportunity in front of me. I know the Lord wants me to do this. I *want* to do this. But I'm afraid of failure. What if it all goes sour?
- I know I should talk to the guys at work about the Lord, but honestly, I'm afraid of rejection. What if they think I'm a weirdo?
- My pastor has asked me to help out in children's church, but I don't know. I'm the type of person who won't even try something if I can't do it perfectly.
- I know that I need to talk to my good friend about what's happening in her life right now, but I'm afraid.
- I've gone through a lot of loss lately, and I prayed for different outcomes than I received. I'm afraid that God doesn't hear my prayers.

God calls us to be people of change, not people who hide. There's a Christmas song that talks about Jesus being meek and mild. I've always thought those words paint the wrong picture of Christ. Maybe there's a good type of meekness that means the same thing as being humble. But when I think of the meaning of the word "mild," it doesn't fit with some of the descriptions of Jesus: He overturned tables, chased demons into pigs, embarrassed his family for all the right reasons, called King Herod the equivalent of a dirty dog, and busted out of a dark tomb. He gave the Pharisees only two choices—repent or kill Him—when He knew full well they would choose the latter. Jesus Christ was more than Braveheart, Rambo, Die Hard and Indiana Jones all put together! Jesus' life was the opposite picture of a person who hides.

I believe there are two kinds of Christians: those who simply cope with life and those who live so that the world they walk through will never be the same again. I call these two types Copers and Catalysts.

The world is in desperate need of Kingdom Catalysts. These are people who exercise violent compassion, violent prayer, violent love and gentleness. Catalysts live to liberate their homes, schools, cities and nations from Satan's control.

Jesus Christ was the ultimate Catalyst in life. He came to Earth refusing to cope with the world as it was. He refused to cope with sin, suffering, hypocrisy, unbelief, demonic activity, injustice, hunger, sickness and poverty. Every day of His ministry He attempted the impossible. He agitated the complacent. He claimed the incredible. He confronted the hypocritical. He challenged the influence of evil. He offered people heaven instead of hell, and ushered in the kingdom of God.

On the other hand, Copers live their lives by following 10 rules that make them feel safe but that are actually lies. Perhaps you know some or all of these insidiously dangerous rules firsthand. These are the Ten Commandments of Coping:

1. *Always be safe.* (That means you never rock the boat. Never. Never. Never.)
2. *Never attempt anything unless you can control the outcome.*
3. *Never risk embarrassing yourself.*
4. *Always make everybody happy.* (God would never want you to do something that makes people mad, now would He?)
5. *If something needs changing, always talk about it with someone who has neither the responsibility nor the authority to do anything about it.* (Never go to the source.)
6. *Always structure your life to fulfill other people's expectations.* (Keep God-given dreams

buried inside. Let others tell you how to live.)

7. *Avoid failure at any cost.* (If at first you don't succeed, destroy all evidence that you tried.)

8. *Listen carefully to pessimists, cynics and worry-warts.* (They're always right.)

9. *Expect the same results that others have had.* (Never believe that God can do a greater thing through your life.)

10. *Never try anything for the first time.*

We need to be people who long to become vessels of the breakthrough God. Being a catalyst is about the incredible privilege of rescuing the hostages of sin and Satan. We need believers who are willing to break through culture barriers, race barriers, gender barriers, language barriers, economic barriers, oppression barriers and poverty barriers to live out the ministry of Jesus Christ today—now. There are 10,000 people groups that still have not heard the gospel. We need people with the courage to show those who are in the most wretched situations in this world that there is a breakthrough God who loves them and is inviting them out of darkness into the celebration of His glorious life.

Did you know that we were all wired to be world changers, not life copers? Satan has never lost sleep over mild people. Jesus was his worst nightmare, and Jesus has given us the invitation to be the same.

But how do we let go of our fears? How do we become Catalysts instead of Copers? How do we position ourselves before God for that one touch from Him that moves us to a breakthrough?

BECOMING A CATALYST

Many people never experience a breakthrough with God because they refuse to let it happen. Why? Fear blocks the path. But fear does not have to rule our lives.

When I look back on my life, there have always been situations that could have kept me from a genuine spiritual breakthrough with God. One of the biggest blockers in my life has been hesitancy. I continually postpone things, hoping things will come together anyway. Here are some examples of what I mean: I asked the Lord into my heart when I was 11, but I thought I was too young to really pursue God in a deep way—so I hesitated. After I graduated from high school, I went to Bible school. My thought was, *When I learn my Bible, then I'll really know God.* So in a sense, I decided to hesitate again to let God touch me like never before. As I entered adulthood and the challenges of life began to set in, it's as if I had contracted the "I'll be happy when" syndrome. Have you ever had that "disease"? It can infect us all the way through life if we don't seek God's touch.

I'll be happy when I get my driver's license. What happens? I get my driver's license and now I have to fight traffic.

I'll be happy when I graduate college. What happens? I graduate, but now I've got to figure out what to do with my life.

I'll be happy when I get married. What happens? Getting married is great, but now I have to learn how to be humble and gracious.

I'll be happy when I retire. Well, I haven't reached that stage of life yet, but I know some sort of challenge will be waiting there, too.

All I'm trying to say is, Stop postponing life! Circumstances will never be tidy and perfect enough. The reason why many of us don't experience spiritual breakthroughs more often is because we fear the changes that a breakthrough can bring. Listen to the voice of God. Stop hesitating. Step up to the plate and swing.

When I was working for Tree Pole—my stick-stacking job—I met an incredible woman named Robin. We dated for five years. I wanted to ask her to marry me, but fear stood in my way. I wanted to be a musician, but every musician I knew was forced to change his career path after he got married. I loved Robin, but I was afraid of abandoning my dreams.

Two years after I moved to California, I asked Robin to marry me. I still hadn't "made it" as a musician, but I needed to stop hesitating. I had to overcome my fears. Fortunately, she said yes. After accepting Christ into my heart, there are two decisions that have been the best I've ever made: marrying Robin is one, and moving to California is the other. Where would I be now if I had continued to hesitate?

When we ask God to break through all of our fears, we're releasing our lives to Him. We no longer clutch, hold and control. Proverbs 3:5-6 encourages us to trust in the Lord with all our hearts, and to lean not on our own understanding, but acknowledge Him in all our ways. What's the promise? That He will make our paths straight. The Lord goes before us, behind us, over us, under us. The Lord leads us, as Psalm 23 says, into green pastures and beside still waters. He restores our souls and guides us in the paths of righteousness for His name's sake. Evil is not ours to fear. The Bible gives us an incredible promise in 1 John 4:4 that greater is He (Jesus) that is in us than he (Satan) that is in the world. This means that because we have Christ, we have nothing to fear. *Nothing.*

I find that declaring God's promises helps put fear in perspective. I remember one time when my mom had a benign growth in her stomach and needed major surgery. We were all afraid for her. I remember going on a prayer walk through my neighborhood, praying—even shouting—God's promises as I walked. The Word of God is a lethal weapon against fear. Here are some of the verses I prayed for my mom:

- "The LORD is my light and my salvation—whom shall I fear? The LORD is the stronghold of my life—of whom shall I be afraid?" (Ps. 27:1).
- "Never will I leave you; never will I forsake you" (Heb. 13:5).
- "You are my hiding place; you will protect me from trouble and surround me with songs of deliverance" (Ps. 32:7).

When we set the Word of God in our minds and hearts, we have a great tool to use against fear. God's promises can come back to us at the strangest times.

One of the instructions God also gives us in times of fear is to remember what He has done in the past. He has been abundantly good and faithful throughout all generations—our generation is no different. Psalm 105:8 reads, "He remembers his covenant forever, the word He commanded, for a thousand generations." Our God is the same God who called a nation out of Abraham and Sarah when they were elderly. God brought the Israelites out of slavery in Egypt to the Promised Land, a land flowing with milk and honey. He took a shepherd boy named David and made him a great king whose wealth and splendor were only topped by his son Solomon. God is the God who healed the blind man and parted the Red Sea. God is the God of the impossible.

And what of God's story in our lives? All blessings flow through Him. He loves us and guides us. He's the One who gives us salvation. He's our Deliverer, our Comforter, our Joy, our Shelter, our Peace, our Helper, our Liberator. He never leaves us. Never forsakes us.

I wrote a song called "We Will Remember," inspired by Nehemiah 9—the passage that describes the works of

God throughout generations.

Here's the chorus:

We will remember, we will remember
We will remember, the works of your hands
We will stop and give you praise
For great is Thy faithfulness.[1]

God broke through my sense of hopelessness and fear when I wrote this song. It was a day when things didn't look so bright. But I was being reminded by God's Word to look back at what He had done. When I saw God's track record throughout history, and especially His hand in the events in my own life, I was filled with courage and hope again.

BREAK THROUGH ALL MY FEARS

March 2006 marks my having lived in California for 20 years. I can honestly say that everything I've ever dreamed of doing has happened. I've traveled to many parts of the world; I've ministered alongside top Christian leaders; I've written songs that have been used globally by the Lord. I mention these things with a sense of humble gratitude. None of it would have happened if I had allowed fear to win the day all those years ago.

The Lord promises that He will give us only what we can bear. When I look back at 2004, I realize now that I was actually internalizing others' heartaches in a way that I wasn't meant to. God deals with each of us according to our needs, and I believe that He personalizes His touch to each one of us—giving us grace and strength in a way that is unique to our individual situations. The same is true when it comes to overcoming fear. Your God is ready to bring light into your darkness in a way that can have meaning only for you.

I want to end this chapter the same way as the previous one: When it comes to overcoming fear, *the real solution is worship*. When we choose to surrender and trust God, even in the midst of confusion, and when we choose to fix our eyes on Jesus, the author of life, that is when God breaks through our fears like never before.

Worship is seeing God for who He is. He's our all in all. Worship is fixing our eyes on Him and not on our situation; it's shifting from the fear of the moment and putting our eyes on the God who is able. It's rediscovering that nothing is too difficult for Him.

PRAYER

Lord, help me say, "Your face is all I see." Let the beauty and strength of who You are outshine the fear and darkness of what is all around me. You are truly bigger, greater, deeper and stronger than my mightiest foe. The darkness is just the backdrop for the unveiling story of how You will reveal Your goodness and faithfulness again. You're my Strong Tower, my Refuge, my Advocate, my Intercessor and my Friend. Draw near to me, Lord, as I turn my eyes on You and let the things of Earth grow dim. Amen.

Note

1. Tommy Walker, "We Will Remember," © 2005.

CHAPTER 4

BREAK THROUGH TO WORSHIP

> Yet a time is coming . . . when
> the true worshipers will worship
> the Father in spirit and truth,
> for they are the kind of
> worshipers the Father seeks.
>
> JOHN 4:23

Have you ever noticed that the call to worship can come when we're least prepared to worship? It's as if a wrestling match is going on in our soul. While our inner person feels apathetic—we're tired, bored, distracted or preoccupied—our inner person is crying out to connect with God. At those times, it helps to declare to yourself and to the Lord, *God, I'm pressing in here. I will worship You. I won't be denied.*

A while ago, I was sitting in my office at the church. It was just another average busy morning. Traffic whizzed by outside on Colorado Boulevard. A stack of e-mails waited for my response. I needed to meet with some of my worship team members about a music project they were creating for children's church. But for some reason, I found it hard to concentrate. It was as if the Lord was telling me to remember Him in a deeper way than usual.

I didn't fight it. I wanted to worship. I pushed back my chair and began to pace around the room. *Lord, here I am. I'm just starting the day with You. This is not a crisis moment in my life—I just want to worship You. What do You want me to see of You this day? Speak to me, Lord, for I long for You.*

I kept pacing and praying. There was nothing— just a sense that God was more than I was giving Him credit for that morning. *Lord, it doesn't matter if You ever touch me again,* I prayed. *You've already brought me so much. Lord, I believe in You. Instead of my usual questions, I offer you my childlike praise.*

Nothing. No voice. No fire. No thunder.

I began to repeat the same line, over and over again. I needed to declare this specific truth to myself. It was a choice of obedience—I would worship God that morning, no matter what:

Lord, I will be Your worshiper.
Lord, I will be Your worshiper.
Lord, I will be Your worshiper.

And God broke through. All the stuff of the morning that had seemed so important became so unimportant in the light of His glory and majesty.

It is so impossible to describe the presence of God, but I'll try. It's a sense of the weight of His glory. It's an awareness that the God of the universe is somehow closer than the breath you breathe. He's inside you, yet all around you. It's the sound of His still, small voice saying that you are His and He is yours. From the very depths of your being you know that it's Him; yet at the same time, so much of who He is remains completely and mysteriously unknowable. For me, on that morning when I said, "I will be Your worshiper," I gained a new sense of His character and wonder. God was high and above all—real and true. He cared about me and loved me. In His presence there was the deep joy that every human heart longs for. God set my spirit free to worship Him that morning.

In this chapter, I want to encourage you to go to that place. We've all had times when the last thing we felt like doing was worship. As a worship leader whose job is to regularly enter God's presence and lead people there, I know the pull all too well. My outer man feels distracted and just about as spiritual as a bump on a log; but my inner man is crying out, desiring to run to God. This understanding has made me very aware of the power of worship. That's why the line in the song "Break Through" is so important—"Break through, that I may worship You." It means: Lord, because You are worthy, because I know it is fitting and right, and because You know what's best for me, *help me worship You.*

When you think about it, the act of worshiping God is amazing. We are given this incredible privilege to actually worship God. The funny thing is, not only is He the focus of our worship, but He is also the one who gives us the motivation to worship in the first place. When we feel a sense of love and adoration toward God, it is He who gives us those feelings to begin with. We worship because He allows us to. We also worship because it's our choice.

Positioning ourselves for a breakthrough in worship, however, may not be as easy as it sounds.

BLOCKERS TO WORSHIP

So many things can keep us from worshiping God. Whether in church or in our prayer closet, we can come with a distracted mind—our thoughts elsewhere, either thinking about a problem or even thinking about trivia.

At our churches there's usually a 20- to 30-minute window built into the service earmarked for worship. For some of us, that's our only worship experience all week long—and even that time can be robbed of meaning by any number of hindrances. We'll be thinking about the music or distracted by someone sitting in front of us or preoccupied with the roast in the oven at home. With all of this and usually much more on our minds, how are we ever supposed to worship the Lord?

I say this carefully, but it's true—worship often takes work. Sometimes it doesn't—perhaps we're on top of a mountain taking in incredible views, and we spontaneously begin to praise God. But most times of worship aren't like that. The mountaintop experiences can be few and far between. We have to choose to worship in those times when it takes some work to go there, such as when we're in church, wondering if we turned the iron off; or when we're in a hospital room beside a dying friend; or when we're driving in our car in heavy traffic. That's where the *work* of worship is. That's when we have a choice. In all of those times, do we acknowledge God for who He truly is?

God gives us a free will to choose what we will do: think about something else, or think about Him? Succumb to pain or doubt or fear, or worship Him? Get lost in debates about music style, or worship Him? Worship requires our will, our surrender, our yielding: *God, You are worthy to be worshiped—so I will worship. Here. Now. I will consciously and deliberately focus my thoughts and attention on the God of wonders.*

For some, that decision will require a change in thinking. When you go to a worship service, it's not like going to a concert where you sit and get entertained. Worship is about participation. I recently led worship at what I would consider a more conservative church. Before we started, one of the worship team members warned me that a lot of the people there only worship in their hearts. What he meant was, Good luck getting anyone to outwardly participate.

Don't get me wrong; I know there are times when the Spirit of God is so strong that you can't really do anything but be still and stand in awe. In times like that, we can be so moved that words cannot leave our mouths because of the sense of awe we feel. Most of the time, I believe that we honor God most when we are willing to give every fiber of our being to express our praise to Him and give Him glory and honor in a very tangible way. God gave us hands and a voice, emotions and a brain. All of these, along with everything else, should be offered up to show Him how much we love Him.

When we worship God in church, it is about a community of believers gathered together to lift up the name of Christ. Certainly the Spirit moves among us, calling us to Him, giving us the ability to declare His praises. Still, it requires our free choice too. We must decide to worship Him. We must decide to fix our thoughts and heart on the Lord.

Equally so, some people are confused about what worship really means. It's easy to think that worship is the same thing as singing—*Okay, we've collected the offering, so now we'll sing a couple more songs.* But singing is only a vehicle for worship—it's a delivery mechanism. Music only helps us focus on the Lord. The challenge is, how do we worship anytime, anywhere, with or without music, in a church service or not, whether we feel like it or not? How do set our thoughts and heart on the Lord at all times?

Worship is ultimately about seeing God for who He is and then responding to Him. Who is God? What is He like? When we see God, we see His amazing attributes and we have no choice but to respond in awe. He is the immortal, invisible, matchless, almighty God. He is always good, always faithful, always true.

"Seeing God" is what Nehemiah invited the Israelites to do during the rebuilding of the walls of Jerusalem: "Stand up and praise the LORD your God, who is from everlasting to everlasting," he says in Nehemiah 9:5. Then he prays this prayer of worship:

> Blessed be Your glorious name, and may it be exalted above all blessing and praise. You alone are the LORD. You made the heavens, even the highest heavens, and all their starry host, the earth and all that is on it, the seas and all that is in them. You give life to everything, and the multitudes of heaven worship you (v. 6).

That's worship—when we focus our mind and heart on who God is, no matter what. Feelings can so easily cloud our way to worship. I recently wrote a song called "When I Don't Know What to Do." It basically says, when I have no answers—when I'm confused, discouraged and afraid—I will lift my hands and worship You. Regardless of whatever is blocking my way, I will be Your worshiper!

The act of worship brings us to a starting point with God like nothing else can. There is an amazing power in worship that frees our hearts to receive God's unexplainable joy, which the world cannot take away, and His peace, which passes understanding. Worship comes from a heart perspective that sees God as greater than our problems and feelings. This perspective allows us to face life, walking by faith and not by sight. "Break through to worship" is the breakthrough that allows us to say, "It is well with my soul," even when all is not well with our circumstances. A breakthrough to worship is when we allow God to proceed. It's when we say, "God, I have nothing to bring but my decision to worship You. I choose. I *let*. God, bring that breakthrough that sets my spirit free to worship You."

I am not trying to give you more "stuff" to do in order to have a better relationship with Christ. That is not what a breakthrough is about at all. Jesus' primary message was not to have us do more or to work harder, which usually only results in a break*down*. Christ's message is to love God with all our heart, soul, mind and strength, and to love our neighbor as ourselves. *Love God and serve others*—it doesn't get more basic than that. In fact, sometimes Christ even told His disciples to get away from it all and get some rest. Worshiping is about a choice to worship God; it's also about resting in Him.

Come where you can enjoy Me and love Me—that's what's truly important, Jesus says to us. That's the message Martha forgot when she criticized her sister, Mary, for sitting at the feet of Jesus and asked Him to make Mary help her.

But Jesus didn't jump to Martha's demands. He didn't tell Mary to work harder. In fact, He said the opposite. He told Martha that only one thing is needed—and Mary had chosen what was better (see Luke 10:38-42).

What is the "one thing" needed? The answer is found in Psalm 27:4. Jesus was probably alluding to this passage by the words He chose to speak to Martha: "One thing I ask of the LORD, this is what I seek: that I may dwell in the house of the LORD all the days of my life, to gaze upon the beauty of the LORD and to seek him in His temple."

Do you see how powerful that passage is? It gives us the solution to every breakthrough we need. The answer is worship—always worship. No matter what our breakthrough blockers are—doubt, fear, pain, guilt—when we always see the Lord, life falls into place. But how do we do that? How do we continually sit at the feet of Jesus? How do we choose both to worship Him and to rest in Him?

The answer may be different from what you think.

WHEN GOD BREAKS THROUGH

The breakthrough to worship is about being involved in a battle—a spiritual battle. We should not be surprised at this. Worship is ultimately about encountering an everlasting God, the Creator of the universe. It's about the light of Christ being placed on the highest lamp stand for the whole world to see. It's about Jesus' fame being spread to more people on Earth. It's about redrawing the lines of God's influence to include new territory. It's about creating an atmosphere of love, hope and faith in the midst of a world of despair.

The enemy doesn't want any of this to happen. This is why the Bible says, "Our struggle is not against flesh and blood, but against the powers of this dark world and against the spiritual forces of evil in the heavenly realms" (Eph. 6:12). We're in a fight, so encountering a struggle should come as no surprise to us. When a professional football team is playing to win the Superbowl, they're not surprised that every attempt forward is a fight. They know that the opposing team wants to knock them down on every play, and they are not discouraged by this. Actually, the struggle is invigorating. They know they're in the midst of something important.

I saw this firsthand in 2003, when I took a team from our church to Zambia. We did a medical outreach and feeding ministry, and every night we held a worship service in a big soccer field in the area. We brought all this gear—really spent a lot of money on equipment for the service. Our aim was to give our best to those who have the least.

The area where we played in the city of N'dola is a very dark place. We constantly felt a spirit of poverty, violence and perversion in this area. The first night, when we started the service, the faces of the people who crowded into the soccer field looked confused. It was as if everybody were saying, "What's this? Music groups never come to our city." That night, and for several nights afterward, we would do about an hour and a half of music; then my brother, Pastor Dale Walker, would preach through an interpreter.

Throughout that entire trip—every single service—worship felt like a battle. Each night, when we started playing, there was the same atmosphere of heaviness throughout the crowd. Then there would be preaching, and people would pray the sinner's prayer to receive Christ. When that happened, we could feel the heaviness lifting. And the people would begin to dance joyfully, their faces like light. We'd do the whole concert over again with a sense of victory in the heavenlies. Every day would begin again at zero with the same spirit of heaviness. When I look back now, that trip was all about declaring the Lordship of Christ and His light in a dark place.

I can now see the experiences of that time as a metaphor for our lives. We may continually experience any number of breakthrough blockers—pain, guilt, fear, doubt. Each day we are faced with the same spirit of heaviness. But the choice to worship is ours to make. When we begin to declare the wonders of the Lord, we position ourselves for a breakthrough. The good news is that Christ has already won the war for us.

I also believe a breakthrough in worship happens when we begin to see others as Christ sees them. Worship and compassion are so closely combined. When we see Christ for who He is, we see others as

His children, wholly and dearly loved.

On another trip, this time to the Philippines, we did a series of worship seminars among the very poorest of the churches. After each seminar, we would invite the people to come forward for prayer. These were people who led worship with some of the most destitute and impoverished people in the country.

I remember one woman who came forward. She looked so beat up, so filthy. She was dressed in rags and had some teeth missing. She stood right in front of me, her matted head bowed, smelling like sweat and dirt. I looked at her and thought, *This woman is the epitome of a forgotten person in the world's eyes—ugly, filthy, old, poor—she has absolutely nothing going for her. She'd be the first person tossed out of the lifeboat. But we asked people to come forward, and she came. And she's standing in front of me. So I need to pray for her.* I confess I hesitated for a moment. I didn't want to touch her. But I laid my hands on her head anyway and began to pray.

What is it about Christ, who sees through to the heart like no other? The minute I touched this woman, I received a window into the love of God like never before. It was like divine electricity racing through my hands. The Lord spoke to me so powerfully, so violently: *You see only the outside, but I look at the heart. This is my princess . . . this is my princess . . . this is my princess.*

Praying for this haggard woman became a moment of incredible worship for me. God showed me more about His character in that instant than I'd seen in a lifetime. No matter how raw, beat up, dirty and ugly we become—we never lose our value to Him. This is the God we serve. His love for us is the radical, unconditional, hold-us-in-His-arms type of love.

To worship is to love each other. When we love each other, we bless the Father.

THE CATCH-22 OF WORSHIP

This chapter, like this whole book, can seem like a Catch-22. We need to worship to receive a breakthrough from God; yet we need a breakthrough from God to begin to worship.

There are so many times when we feel lost and far from God; but after choosing to worship Him, everything comes right. At other times, God swoops into our hearts and into the circumstances of our lives and shows us incredible windows into His character. At those times, we have no choice but to praise Him.

The good news is this: God is faithful. When we make just the smallest step of obedience toward Him—when we just lean in His direction—God is so ready to touch us in life-changing ways.

The "how to" aspect of this chapter is this: When we worship and nothing seems to happen, that's when we just go into obedience mode. In other words, we don't leave and we don't give up; we just keep showing up, because our breakthrough is on the way! We position ourselves before the Lord and wait.

Unfortunately, I know a lot of sad stories of people who never broke through simply because they gave up and left.

Breakthroughs can come fast or they can come slow. Either way, our call is to obedience. *I'll be your worshiper anyway, God. My choice is to declare Your praises, above what I'm feeling right now, beyond my experiences. You are faithful. You are good. Break through, Lord Jesus, break through that I may worship You.*

PRAYER

God, You are the breakthrough God. My only hope is to turn to You—no matter what I'm feeling or going through. This moment, I choose to worship You. Amen.

Lord, I surrender all
To Your strong and faithful hand;
In everything I will give thanks to You,
I'll just trust Your perfect plan.

When I don't know what to do
I'll lift my hands
When I don't know what to say
I'll speak Your praise
When I don't know where to go
I'll run to Your throne
When I don't know what to think
I'll stand on Your truth
When I don't know what to do

Lord I surrender all
Though I'll never understand
All the mysteries around me
I'll just trust your perfect plan
As I bow my knee
Send Your perfect peace
Send Your perfect peace, Lord
As I lift my hands
Let Your healing come
Let Your healing come to me[1]

Note

1. Tommy Walker, "When I Don't Know What to Do," © 2005.

CHAPTER 5

BREAK THROUGH PAIN

> And the God of all grace, who
> called you to His eternal glory
> in Christ, after you have suffered
> for a little while, will himself
> restore you and make
> you strong, firm and steadfast.
>
> 1 PETER 5:10

One afternoon about six years ago, I bent down to pick up a piece of music gear—a digital recorder sitting on a low coffee table in a friend's studio. I had to lean forward to pick up the recorder, and when I did, I knew that nothing felt like it should.

When I straightened up, recorder in my arms, that one crazy motion was all it took. *Ouch.*

Everything was changed.

Some years earlier, I had felt the agonizing pain of throwing my back out—but this pain wasn't like that time. *That* pain got better; this pain made me hope that if I just lay down it would go away. Trouble was, it didn't. It was kind of a twisting, burning sensation. Not excruciating but pretty much never ending. The pain just became stronger and stronger. Something seriously wrong had occurred.

I saw doctors and chiropractors, did exercises and stretches and, for a short time, took medication and pain relievers. Months went by and nothing helped. I was finally diagnosed with fractured vertebrae and a slightly bulging disc in my lower back. The doctors think the actual injury happened many years earlier. My picking up the recorder was simply the final straw. Welcome to my new life of pain, which I still feel today.

I don't tell that story to get sympathy (and I'm not looking for any advice—so please don't send me any pills or home remedies!), but only to show that I'm someone who can identify with constant, daily pain. I've tried everything. Sometimes the pain in my back eases up for a few weeks. Sometimes stretches are helpful. But mostly, it feels like someone is stabbing me— in a continual, nagging twist—all day long.

I've learned to just deal with it. I know that I can't pick up my kids anymore. They've learned that they can't run and jump into my arms. Every morning I ice my back while I drive my boys to school.

That's what constant pain is like—it rearranges your life. I realize there are people who live with more pain than I do—at least I still have a lot of mobility. But every one of us, I believe, has some sort of pain that we deal with on a constant basis. It may not be the physical pain of a hurt back; it may be emotional pain or spiritual pain; it may be the pain of remembering something, or the pain of a relationship gone sour.

The question is, Can we ever come to peace with our pain? I'm not saying that we don't acknowledge it; but do we get to the place where it doesn't impede our relationship with God? It's human nature when we're in pain to run anywhere else but to Him. But God has the power to break through our pain. Breakthroughs may look different for different people. God may choose to heal. He may choose not to heal but to give more grace to cope with the pain. He may choose to help us deal with the situation so that we become more empathetic. He may choose some course of action that we could not have dreamed up.

No matter what the cause of our pain, how can we position ourselves to receive a breakthrough in this area? Pain can be a huge blocker that sets up a barrier between us and God. How can we run to God, and not away from Him, in the midst of our pain?

WITHIN THE PAIN

Pain can stop us cold—spiritually, that is. And that's a problem. When we're in pain, often the first thing we do is question God—Why do I have this pain? Why is God letting it continue? It can be very difficult to worship God in the midst of sorrow and suffering.

What kind of pain is in your life?

Some pain is obvious. There's no way we can't know it's not there. Some pain is more subtle. It sneaks up on us. Sometimes we stuff down the pain. Sometimes our pain prompts us to go to a substance or harmful activity, seeking relief.

We are in pain when we begin sentences with:

- If only this hadn't happened to me, Lord . . .
- When I look back on my life, this experience is only one dark area . . .
- Let me tell you about something I really, really regret . . .

- I just feel hopeless and helpless about . . .
- This sure didn't turn out the way I thought it would . . .

My mom, Eileen Walker, has experienced a lot of physical pain. In 1982, she was diagnosed with a severe form of glaucoma and other eye-related conditions that robbed her of her ability to see normally. Mom's vision increasingly diminished, and her eyes became highly sensitive to light. She needed to cover all of the windows in the house with dark contact paper. She literally became a prisoner of darkness. Her eyes also brought her daily, unyielding pain.

During those dark days, Mom had a decision to make—whether she articulated it in these words, I don't know. But it's the same decision we all need to make when we're in pain: *Will I run to God or run away from Him?*

In spite of the pain, Mom chose the Lord. Every day she made it her aim to fix her thoughts on God. She continually surrendered her will to Him and focused on His promises and attributes.

During one painful moment, she remembers describing to Jesus the pain she was feeling. It was the beginning of an experience that yielded an amazing breakthrough.

Are You here, Lord? she prayed. *Are You with me in the midst of this situation?*

Almost audibly, God spoke to her: *Yes. Absolutely. I'm here in this pain.*

Okay, Lord, I embrace You in this situation, in this pain. If You are indeed here, then I can make it. With Your presence, I'll be all right. Thank You.

Then the Lord gave her another insight—one of the most valuable she has ever received.

I'm in the pain, God said to her, *but there is no pain in Me.*

There is no pain in God. God is with us in the pain, but the pain is not *of* Him.

That was it. That was the true breakthrough Mom had been searching for—a greater knowledge of her Lord and Savior. God's character was all about truth and goodness, not sorrow and suffering. God could be found in pain, but pain was not of Him.

There was more. Much more. During a church service, the power of God came over Mom and her pain subsided. I was with her that day, and what a celebration we had! When she returned home, she turned on the lights and opened the curtains. She was

cured. She couldn't believe it. She went to her doctors, who took X-rays and concluded that a miracle
had happened. Mom returned to the world of light
where she has served God without eye pain ever since.

Miraculous physical healing doesn't come to
everybody. It hasn't come to me and my back pain.
But God can break through pain in a variety of ways.
And when He does break through, His presence
changes the whole dynamic of the experience. His
presence may instantly change the molecular structure of a diseased condition as it did for my mom.
Or His presence may change the perspective of a
hopeless heart bound by bitterness. His presence
may convey hope or endurance or empathy or wisdom or grace.

The apostle Paul's experience of pain is a good
example of God's giving grace. Paul had some sort of
painful condition—we don't know exactly what it
was. Three times Paul prayed that the Lord would
take away the affliction, but the Lord gave him this
message instead: "My grace is sufficient for you; for
my power is made perfect in weakness" (2 Cor. 12:9).

The bad news is that pain can be very real in our
lives. The good news is that pain doesn't need to have
the last word. Pain can make us run to God or away

from Him. When we run to Him, He may take the pain away or He may show us something completely different. God is always there with us in our pain, but there is no pain in Him.

If you're in pain today, right now, what practical steps can you take to position yourself for a break-through from the Lord? How do you worship Him in the midst of your trouble?

LISTEN TO GOD

A big part of breaking through to God in the midst of pain is learning to hear His voice. When we hear Him, we gain a greater glimpse of His purposes. We may not have more specific understanding of our situation, but we'll understand more that His ways are always good.

Learning to listen can be like any other discipline. It just takes practice. The main reasons that we don't hear Him are because we don't believe that He speaks, or we're too busy talking, or we're constantly filling our lives with the noise and busyness of the world.

Years ago, when I was single, my oldest brother, Jerry, asked me to house-sit for him. Jerry works as a real-estate agent, and this was one of the houses that was on the market. Every night I came to this house alone. There was no TV, no radio, no phone, no magazines, no newspapers—nothing. With nothing to distract me, I began to read the classic devotional book *The Pursuit of God*, by A. W. Tozer. Every chapter ends with a prayer. I got on my knees and prayed those prayers fervently. After praying, I would be still and listen. What did I hear?

The humming of a fridge. The distant buzz of traffic. The creaks of a house settling at night after a warm day.

Mostly I just heard silence.

But in that silence, God began to speak to me like never before. He communicated His presence. Verses came to me that I had memorized years before. God's attributes of love, faithfulness, kindness and mercy spoke to me in new ways. God was real. He was alive, and He cared for me as His son. This went on for about a month. It was as if I were on an adventure and couldn't wait to see where God and I would go next.

Since then, I've tried to make listening to God a consistent discipline in my devotional life. It's as simple as this: After reading from the Bible, I allow time—say 5 to 10 minutes—to be still. My focus is on whatever the Lord may want to impress on me. I may start this time by saying, "Lord, speak to me. Be my teacher, my counselor, my friend."

Then I wait . . .

At first, I only had faith to believe that God was saying something simple to me—such as that He loved me. But as time went on, I sensed that God would speak more specific things to me. I can remember trying to make a big decision in my life. After reading the story of Jesus walking on water, I heard the Lord say, *Tommy, you're living in the boat of indecision, and until you take a step of faith and get out of the boat, you will never be able to see what I can do for you.*

I'm always hesitant to share these types of things, because I don't want to teach technique. The God we serve is alive and ever moving in fresh ways, so I definitely don't want to put Him in a box. There's another danger also—people can claim to "hear" the voice of God and then go out and do all sorts of crazy things because of what they claim to hear. The primary way that God speaks to us is through His Word—the Bible. Apart from that, any true voice of God we hear will always line up with Scripture. *Always.* If the voice we hear doesn't agree with Scripture, then it's not the voice of God.

What is God telling you in the midst of your pain?

God may be telling you that some good is coming from your pain. Or perhaps He may be telling you that your pain is being used as discipline. Scripture says that God disciplines those He loves (see Heb. 12:6). It's forever a mystery what side the pain is on—who did it come from? The evil one or our own mistakes? Or was our pain allowed by God for a purpose? No matter what the source of our pain, it can be used for God's glory. Discipline never feels pleasant at the time; but God can use it to make us more like Him and to reveal new aspects of who He is—previously unknown treasures of His character.

I've written a lot of worship songs in the midst of pain. It's as if God somehow reveals Himself to me in ways I would have never imagined had I not experienced pain. Pain ushers in a compassion within me for others that I wouldn't have except for the pain.

I experience a type of hope I wouldn't have without my pain. It's the hope that knows my pain will someday end—maybe here on Earth, maybe when I'm with the Lord in heaven. This insight is similar to when I had all those horrible jobs before I moved to California—I knew I could stand the pain because someday the pain would end. People so desperately need this kind of hope. A person can put up with anything if he or she knows it's not forever. Even in the midst of pain, we have the certain hope that someday God will release us from it. Because of that knowledge, God's grace is enough for me today.

BREAK THROUGH ALL PAIN

It's far too easy to put a happy face on pain and leave it at that. But that's not what I want to say at all. I don't want to sugarcoat the reality of pain. But I will say that much good can come from it.

When we learn to listen to the Lord, He can tell us things through our pain that we might not be able to hear otherwise. Sometimes there is great purpose in pain. Sometimes pain can move us forward out of a desperate situation. Sometimes it warns us that something is wrong, and we change only because of the pain.

But the truth is also that real people are involved in pain. And pain hurts. When I look at my friend Jeff Lams who recently lost his daughter to leukemia, I don't want to try and "solve" his pain in any way. I don't want to share any "happy" verses with him or try to cheer him up. I just want to be willing to sit with him and cry.

The big picture is that God can redeem pain. I know that sometimes we can be hurting too badly to see the big picture. But it's true that God can use pain for His glory. When my sister's son, Charlie, died from a congenital heart defect at age 13, there was so much pain surrounding that situation. We will never understand why Charlie had to suffer, or why many injustices happen to innocent children. Yet we can be overwhelmed by God's amazing, redeeming power to take tragedies and injustices in our lives and turn them into precious, eternal victories.

Charlie's Lunch Ministry began as an expression of the grief my sister and her husband felt at the loss of their son. Charlie was always such a compassionate child—he was always giving his lunch away at school. After Charlie died, my sister began feeding hungry children in Guatemala, where they served as missionaries, as a remembrance of the lunch she would have prepared for Charlie every day. Today, Charlie's Lunch Ministry serves meals to thousands of children each month in Mexico, Guatelmala, El Salvador and India.

When we're in pain, God gives us a grace and a revelation unique to our situation and to who we are. God is the God of the one lost lamb. How God works with me will be different from how God works with you. Remember earlier when I said I was a desperately shy kid while growing up? I think that if you saw me in my junior high school yearbook, I would have been the kid with the title "Most likely *not* to succeed." Sure, there was pain in being shy. But because of that pain, I stayed inside a lot, playing guitar, and God used that shyness to produce in me a talent he was later going to use for His glory. If I had been a popular kid, I doubt that I would have sat in my room practicing guitar to the extent that I did. God used what was wrong and turned it into something right and good.

I wonder today how He will use my back pain—or any of the other pains I experience. It's not for me to understand just yet, but only to trust Him. And what about you? What will He use your pain for? Don't forget that during creation, God spoke light into the darkness. There had to be a death before there could be a resurrection. The lights of the movie theater have to go out before the story can begin. Pain doesn't have to mean the end; it can be the very thing that ushers in a new beginning!

PRAYER

O Lord, You know what pain I'm experiencing right now. You were rejected and tortured beyond anything that I will ever know. In Isaiah 53:3, You are described as "a man of sorrows, and familiar with suffering." What a comfort to me that You understand pain and know it better than any other! So I pray again: Help me break through all my pain. Rescue me—deliver me in whatever way You choose, that I may worship You. I choose to worship You now—here—in spite of what I'm feeling. I declare to myself and to the world around me that You are good. You are kind. You are loving. You are faithful. I may not understand Your purpose in this pain, but I trust that You have a purpose. Amen.

CHAPTER 6

BREAK THROUGH GUILT AND SHAME

> The LORD longs to be
> gracious to you.
>
> ISAIAH 30:18

I was alone in a hotel room after leading worship at Promise Keepers when temptation hit.

How ironic. I had just finished leading 50,000 men in declaring our allegiance to the Lord of all righteousness; the Houston Astrodome had become a temple of the Lord's glory earlier that same evening. But here I was just a few hours later, remote control inches away from my hand, a voice on my shoulder saying, "Some channel surfing is what you need right now."

It's always *after* a spiritual high that we get tested or can actually succumb to a temptation that leads to sin. When we're alone and tired—either spiritually or physically—that's a prime time for the evil one to make us a target. This was the seventh or eighth Promise Keepers event in which I had participated that year. I was exhausted.

I knew that all I had to do was flip on the TV and it wouldn't be long before I stumbled across something I had no business watching. I was sure of it. This is not a habitual sin for me, but men—every guy will know what I'm talking about here—are *always* susceptible in the battle of lust.

I remember making a very conscious decision that night to not turn on the TV. I picked up my guitar and began to sing back to God all that I knew to be true about Him. I began to write a song—"That's Why We Praise Him." The first verse and chorus go like this:

He came to live, live a perfect life
He came to be the living word our light
He came to die so we'd be reconciled
He came to rise to show His pow'r and might

That's why we praise Him
That's why we sing

That's why we offer Him our everything
That's why we bow down and worship this King
'Cause He gave His everything[1]

As I wrote and worshiped, God broke through. His presence was so real—so holy. I was not going to fall to temptation that night in the hotel room. I couldn't allow that to happen. I didn't want the potential guilt and shame of that experience to clog my relationship with the Lord.

Here's the funny thing about that song. Out of the hundreds of worship songs I've written over the years, the song I wrote that night in the hotel room—"That's Why We Praise Him"—is the most widely sung song I've written. It's been sung all over North America; it has been translated into different languages and has gone all over the world. I've even seen a video of people singing it in Siberia. They were all bundled up in their parkas in a tiny Orthodox church. A Russian worship leader was up front leading the congregation with stiff choir conductor-like motions. It was absolutely great!

That's a story about the opposite of what I'm talking about. It's a story of those little secret decisions we make that can end up being big—either good decisions or bad decisions.

On one hand, we can fall to temptation and let the guilt and shame of our sins keep God from blessing us. This results in our thinking that we're too horrible to come to God. Too unworthy. How could God ever love us and call us by name?

On the other hand, when we're completely sold out to Him, He can use our smallest decisions in big ways. That night in the hotel room, the choice was mine. I could either pick up the remote control or pick up my guitar. If I had chosen the former, a song that's been so widely used by the Lord would not have been written.

I wish I could say that all the decisions I've made in my life have been to turn to God and not away from Him. But that's not the case. The Bible says that all are sinners. We've all fallen short of the glory of God (see Rom. 3:23). And when we do sin, what is our response? Can God still break through our guilt and shame? That's what this chapter is about.

TANGLED AND TWISTED

Let's face it, sin happens. The prophet Jeremiah described the heart as deceitful and desperately wicked (see Jer. 17:9). All of us have hearts that have lied to us, that have chosen to believe things about God, about ourselves, and about this world that aren't true. In 2 Corinthians 4:4, Paul says that the god of this world has blinded our eyes.

Sin entangles our lives in a number of ways. Sometimes sin is purposeful, habitual—we may even not want to break its hold on us. Sometimes sin is occasional, a slipup, a mistake. We feel a sense of sorrow and want to be free. Other times, sin becomes so powerful in our lives that it overtakes us. We become trapped in an addiction. It can seem like there is no way out.

What happens when we sin? There are consequences. One consequence may be feelings of guilt and shame. Those feelings can be good if they cause us to turn from our sins. The answer to guilt and shame is simple: confession and repentance. There's a breakthrough power in confession like nothing else. Sin is all about hiddenness and secrets. It's about keeping everything in the dark. But when we confess our sins to one another, we illuminate them with the light.

One of the saddest things about hidden sin is that it alienates us from God, who loves us, and it also alienates us from the people who love us. It's the opposite of breakthrough. It keeps us living in a prison. Repentance is the key that unlocks our prison door of sin. Repentance is the U-turn we make in humble obedience. When we repent, we agree that His ways are better than our ways—His is the only road that leads to life.

Confession and repentance can be difficult. We need to humble ourselves, admit our frailties and ask forgiveness of the Lord—and sometimes ask forgiveness of those we have wronged. We may also need to pay some sort of compensation—make things right—if we've inflicted damage on someone or something. That takes guts. But we need to do it. We need to leave the familiarity of our sin and step out in courage. On the other side of confession and repentance, there is joy, freedom and peace. David says in Psalm 32:3-5: "When I kept silent, my bones wasted away. . . . Then I acknowledged my sin . . . and you forgave the guilt of my sin."

After we've confessed our sins, feelings of guilt and shame can plague us if we still feel that we're too horrible for God to want a relationship with us. But that's the voice of the enemy coming to kill, steal and destroy. With false guilt and shame, it's easy to feel as if we don't deserve a touch from heaven. We may consciously know that we're forgiven, but still we feel dirty, cheapened, far away from God. Our unconfessed sin and our feelings of false guilt and shame can be blockers to receiving a breakthrough from God.

I'm reminded of a time when some pastors in the Philippines took us to tour the Manila dump—home to tons upon tons of trash and refuse, and the people who live there. That may sound strange that we were touring the dump, but this was no vacation—not for us, and not for the thousands of people who call the Manila dump their home.

Picture the worst conditions you can imagine: acres and acres of trash piled high—up to 10 stories or more. Within the trash, poor people have built places to live, sometimes out of cardboard, parts of signs or plywood. The "nicer" shacks are scraped together from cinder blocks. Paths have been carved through the garbage to make "roads" that remain wet from sewer water flowing through them.

This place is the face of extreme poverty. Children, all who are in various stages of malnutrition, walk around barefoot with cuts and scrapes on their feet and knees. Many have respiratory tract infections from living in the damp. A variety of other diseases are rampant. Bad smells and decay are everywhere. Most shacks are just one room, so there's never any privacy.

Perversion is common, as is violence. There is such a feeling of hopelessness. Nothing will ever change.

Here's the absolute crazy thing. The pastors told us that sometimes, even when hope is available—even when there's a chance for people to leave the dump—people will sometimes say no. They'll resist change and actually *choose to stay*. The dump is all they know. There's comfort in the familiar. It's a terrible existence, but at least they know what to expect.

Can you imagine choosing to *not* leave a dump?

There may be a parallel to our own lives here. How many times do we choose to stay in the familiar "bad" instead of going to the new "good"? Sin is as insidious as a Third World dump, but when freedom is offered to us, we cling to our trash instead. Either we don't believe that something better exists, or we don't have the courage to venture into the unknown.

Guilt and shame do not have to master us. The Holy Spirit can awaken us to our senses and move us from slavery to Sonship, from addiction to sobriety, from alienation into acceptance. There is a loving heavenly Father waiting for us to come home. He's waiting to wrap His arms around us, no matter how wretched our lives have been.

Sin is real—that's the bad news. Our hearts have darkness clinging to them—covering and suffocating who we really are, who we are meant to be. But there is good news, too. The Spirit of God has been sent by Jesus to convict the world of sin, righteousness and judgment. He literally hovers over our lives. Forgiveness is ours. There is no condemnation for those who are in Christ Jesus. When we allow God's forgiveness and love to break into our hearts by the work Christ did for us on the cross, we will never be the same again.

THE REMEDY FOR A DARKENED HEART

The secret to breaking through all our sins, including the residue of guilt and shame, lies in our relationship with the Lord. I've said it before, but I need to say it again: This book is not meant to be some sort of three-step self-help book. I'm not a counselor, and that's not the type of solution I know anything about.

The real solution is as simple and (sometimes) as difficult as this: *We find breakthrough in worship.* After we have confessed and repented of our sins, we must once again fix our eyes on Christ, on His promises and character. When we do this, our lives fall into place. The answer begins with repentance but should always end in worship.

I remember a time when I was struck with the sin of jealousy. I had just started leading worship at Christian Assembly, and all the guys in the church went on a men's retreat at Lake Arrowhead in California's San Bernardino Mountains.

Being a full-time worship leader was still new to me. While I was studying at the Musicians Institute in Hollywood, I had started volunteering at the church. My time expanded from a part-time position to a full-time one. I was the worship leader now at Christian Assembly. So I reasoned that I should be leading worship at the men's retreat. (By the way, I don't believe that today.)

But I was new, and there were other gifted musicians and worship leaders at the church (there still are today), and our senior pastor had asked one of the other guys to lead worship at this retreat. The other guy was a gifted musician and singer, and he did a great job. After he was done, our pastor stood in front of everybody and said something like: "You know, I don't think there's anybody I would rather listen to than [and here he named the other guy who was leading worship]." All I could think was: *What am I, chopped liver?!*

This other guy got credit when I didn't. I felt insecure. I felt resentful. There's no other way to say it. My envy could have kept me down. It could have blocked my relationship with the Lord. That type of pride can destroy you if you let it—you can really make some ridiculous decisions when you think you need to be in charge but aren't meant to be.

The Bible contains stories for every situation in life, and it certainly contains some about jealousy. For example, when the young shepherd boy, David, killed the giant, Goliath, there was singing throughout the city of Jerusalem in praise of David. The celebration should have been for King Saul—he was the leader of the army. But when the king saw the celebration, he was instantly jealous, and the horrible seed of jealousy that was sown that day grew into a stubborn and prolific weed. Throughout the book of 1 Samuel, we read of a man whose life and decisions became increasingly ruled by resentment, suspicion and mistrust. On one occasion, Saul hurled a spear at David. On another, Saul led an entire army to destroy David. Saul ended up falling on his own sword, dying with his life in ruins, all because he turned his heart away from the

Lord. Saul let the sin of jealousy, among other sins, build and fester until it conquered him, devouring his life.

That could have been me—not that I was about to fall on my sword, but what I needed during that men's retreat was a breakthrough. I could sense God's immediate lack of comfort with my envious heart. I needed to yield, to surrender, to *let*. I remember it well, sitting there after that worship session. It was a Holy Spirit moment. It was as if God were saying to me: *Are you going to celebrate this guy's gift, or are you going to resent it?* God could release me from my jealousy. The question was, Could He trust me with others being better than me?

So I yielded. I prayed, *Thank You, God; thank You for putting such exceptional gifts into this person.* I confessed envy to the Lord and asked for His forgiveness. Right there I bowed my head and began to pray. I let this gifted friend of mine lead me in worship. I thanked God for being such an understanding Father to His children—He knows the frailties of our hearts. And I worshiped God for not allowing me to stay in my sin. God cares about me enough to not let me wallow in envy.

Do you long for a breakthrough from God? Do you long to be set free from guilt and shame? Then worship Him. See Him for who He is. Immerse your-

self in the goodness and greatness of an amazing
God. Claim His promises and pray them back to Him.
Say, *Lord, You say in Scripture that* (fill in the blank with
the verses you read). *So now I'm holding You to this.*

What types of passages are we talking about?

- *"Have mercy on me, O God, according to your un-
  failing love; according to your great compassion blot
  out my transgressions. Wash away all my iniquity
  and cleanse me from my sin"* (Ps. 51:1).
- *"If we confess our sins, he is faithful and just and will
  forgive us our sins and purify us from all unrigh-
  teousness"* (1 John 1:9).
- *"'Come now, let us reason together,' says the LORD.
  'Though your sins are like scarlet, they shall be as
  white as snow; though they are red as crimson, they
  shall be like wool'"* (Isa. 1:18).

It's as simple (and complex!) as that. God is ready
and willing to restore to us the joy of our salvation.
He will grant us willing spirits to sustain us. He will
never cast us away from His presence. He cleanses us
and purifies our lives.

If you are seeking a breakthrough from guilt and
shame, worship Him! Pray for the Holy Spirit's power

to overcome evil. Rest in His promise that your sin is removed.

THE GOD WHO KNOWS NO RESENTMENT

Just as it's not God's will for us to live guilt-ridden lives, it *is* God's will for us to live lives of freedom. God wants us to live breakthrough lives. That's His desire. Everything He brings into our lives, He brings for this purpose—*to set us free*. God wants us free to worship Him, free to minister to others, free to be conformed to the image of His Son, free to enjoy Him forever. Anything that is God-ordained is for the purpose of our freedom.

Have you ever considered how easily God doesn't hold resentment for us? We may have muddied our lives considerably. We may have clogged our relationship with Him by our hard hearts. But how easily He turns to us.

I saw a good picture of this the other night with my eight-year-old daughter, Emmie. She and her four-year-old sister, Eileen, share the same bedroom (and bed) by choice. It's a good thing. They get along quite well for siblings and really enjoy each other's company.

Whenever I put Emmie and Eileen to bed, they start playing a game called "The Holding-On Game." Basically, it's just their way to keep me with them longer to postpone my tucking them in for the night. I get up to leave, and they try to hold on. Sometimes I have to get stern so that the game will end; but inevitably they will get me laughing, and then they get too riled up. But all in all, it's a great time of just being together.

The other night, I had to discipline Emmie for something. I don't even remember what. The discipline was over, but I was tired. So when I tucked her into bed, I just kissed her goodnight and left. No Holding-On Game that night. I could tell she wasn't happy with me. Even though she deserved discipline, the discipline was over by then, and maybe I was being too harsh with her.

A few minutes went by, and I got to thinking. Truthfully, I had made my daughter sad. Now I needed to ask her forgiveness. Before I could creep back into her room, I heard her call for me: "Daddy . . . Daddy . . . Daddy . . ."

I went to her and got down close, on her level. I could see that Eileen was already asleep beside her.

"What's wrong?" I asked.

Quicker than anything, Emmie whispered: "Daddy, I love you."

What a beautiful picture of someone who doesn't hold resentment against me.

There is another Someone who doesn't hold resentment against us. God forgives easily. He is always a gracious God, slow to anger, abounding in love.

PRAYER

O Lord, truly You are wonderful. When we have
gone astray, You welcome us back with open
arms. How quick Your forgiveness. How thorough
Your cleansing. Break through all my guilt
and my shame. Break through like
only You can do. Amen

Note
1. Tommy Walker, "That's Why We Praise Him." © 1999 Doulos
   Publishing/We Mobile Music. All rights reserved. Used by
   permission.

CHAPTER 7

BREAK THROUGH LIKE ONLY YOU CAN DO

> For you created my inmost being;
> you knit me together in my
> mother's womb. I praise you
> because I am fearfully and
> wonderfully made.
>
> PSALM 139:13-14

Billy Graham and his wife, Ruth, were reportedly traveling in Switzerland many years ago when Ruth walked into a jewelry store and fell in love with a watch. She bought the watch and gave it to Billy as a gift. Billy loved the watch, and it meant even more to him because Ruth had given it to him as a present and a reminder of their travels together.

Several months later, back in the States, the watch stopped. Billy took it to a jewelry store whose owner examined it and then shook his head. "Sorry," the owner said. "We can't fix that watch here. You'll have to take it back to where you bought it."

Billy gulped. Switzerland wasn't just around the block. Fortunately, a few years later, he and Ruth were able to return to Switzerland. They remembered the broken watch and located the very jewelry store where the watch was purchased.

"Can you fix it?" asked Billy, with a concerned look on his brow.

"No problem," said the Swiss jewelry store owner, a minute or two after examining the watch. "We know everything there is to know about that watch. We made it here."

No one can fix us like our Creator can. God knows how every fiber of our being operates. He understands perfectly how our souls and bodies are linked together. Only He—the One who made us—can fix us and ultimately break through to our lives.

When we long for lasting change, and our souls cry out for breakthrough, it's easy for us to cry out to anyone else but God. We cram our lives with things that only mask our pain in the short term—busyness, addictive habits, a never-ending stream of mindless entertainment. These things never bring lasting satisfaction or change. They only postpone the possibility of receiving the breakthrough power of God in our lives.

When we cry out for breakthrough, the only Person we must cry out to is the Lord. Only God, who knows every mystery; who understands all of nature and science; who sees the past, present and future; who knew us before the foundations of time began; who formed the very universe we live in—only He is able to bring true breakthrough. He has all the power. He keeps the planets spinning around the sun. He's the inventor of electricity. He dreamt up gravity. He gives motion to our brain waves. He formed the intricacies of the human genome. He is the God behind all and through all and in all. He is the breakthrough God.

This is the same breakthrough God that David prays to in Psalm 25:15, acknowledging Him as the only, ultimate solution: "My eyes are ever on the LORD, for *only He* will release my feet from the snare" (emphasis added).

This is the same breakthrough God in Micah 2:12-13, who is compared to a shepherd making a safe passageway for his sheep: "One *who breaks open the way* will go up before them; they will *break through* the gate and go out" (emphasis added).

This is the same breakthrough God whom David talks about in 2 Samuel 5:20: "As waters break out, the LORD has broken out against my enemies before me." David names the place where God accomplishes a mighty victory "Baal-Peazim," which means "the Lord broke through."

God can do this for us. He can bring a breakthrough like no one else can.

ANYWHERE BUT TO GOD

What is it about our humanness that makes us choose to run anywhere but to God? The children of Israel witnessed firsthand example after example of direct involvement with God: He parted the Red Sea for them; He made water gush from a rock when they were thirsty; He guided them by a pillar of cloud by day and a pillar of fire by night. Yet time after time, the Israelites strayed from Him. Why were they so quick to run to other gods?

Why do we often do the same?

Think for a moment. In our usual patterns of living, what are some of the first things we typically turn to when something goes wrong? We may check our finances or phone a friend or reach for a bottle or cry. Our "first solutions" often reveal something about where we put our primary trust.

My father-in-law, Bob Mack, is a great example of someone who prays instantly about almost everything. He'll be driving by a car accident and say out loud, "Lord, we just pray for the people involved in this—for their comfort and protection." Or he'll walk outside and say, "Lord, thanks for this amazing day."

I always want to be like that, but my tendency is to want to figure out life on my own first. But my father-in-law's example models someone who makes God the first option.

When I say that we need to go to the Lord first, I'm knocking other legitimate "cures." I go to the doctor when I'm sick. I get help with my taxes every year. I'm not against it if people need medication or surgery or counseling or to read self-help books. The Lord may choose to work through those methods of healing, guidance and direction.

But there will come a time, a place and a circumstance in everyone's life when no human solution will ever be possible. At those times, there will be only One who is strong enough, big enough, wise enough, bright enough to turn to. That's the Lord. So why not turn to Him always?!

The God we serve is the breakthrough God. He can do the impossible. Just listen to some of these true stories of breakthrough.

A BREAKTHROUGH GOD AT WORK

My friend Linda McCrary sings on our church's worship team and has done several recordings with me.

In the 1980s, she was heavily involved in the music industry in Hollywood. She worked as a session musician and sang backup for a variety of artists, such as Eric Clapton, Elton John, Michael Jackson and Stevie Wonder.

During those years, Linda experienced a lot of disappointment with the music industry, as well as with her life. She got involved with alcohol and cocaine at the craziest of California parties, and her life crumbled. She was a Christian, but during those years she left her faith behind.

At one point, she was homeless, living in one of the parks in Los Angeles. Her self-worth was at the zero level. She wanted to die. She was arrested and went to jail twice, and then went back to the park to live.

The funny thing is, even when she was strung out on cocaine and sleeping on park benches, she still talked to other homeless people and addicts about the Lord. One of the addicts she witnessed to, a former airline pilot, proved to be a catalyst in her breakthrough.

One night, when the pilot was trying to get his life back together, he sought out Linda, who was staying in a hotel room. He knocked on the door seeking his own deliverance and begged her to read something from the Bible and to pray for him. Linda opened the bedside table drawer, found the Bible placed there by the Gideons, and began to read Psalm 40 to him.

> I waited patiently for the LORD;
> He turned to me and heard my cry.
> He lifted me out of the slimy pit,
> Out of the mud and mire;
> He set my feet on a rock
> And gave me a firm place to stand,
> He put a new song in my mouth,
> A hymn of praise to our God (vv. 1-3).

As Linda read that portion of Scripture, she began to cry. Very suddenly—supernaturally—God broke through. Healing came to her heart as she felt the amazing love, grace and forgiveness of Jesus Christ. Deliverance came to her immediately, and she was instantly healed of her addictions. That was September 8, 1989. She hasn't relapsed since.

Linda's message today is that God wants to heal every one of us. Satan wants to create illusions to keep us trapped, but God is bigger and more powerful. Only He, the Author of our faith, can breathe life back into our souls. He can bring hope again like no one else can do.

————

Sam and Gracie, a couple at my brother Dale's church, had a marriage of sorrows. In spite of having three beautiful children together, they rarely talked as a couple and spent most of their energies avoiding each other. A callused layer of hurt and disappointment seem to cover their hearts. Although married, they lived separate lives.

When Gracie first came to talk with Pastor Dale, she had only recently learned of Sam's unfaithfulness to their marriage vows and was crushed. She was desperate for a solution that afternoon, and she prayed for God to do what only He could do—to give her hope and the ability to go on.

Sam continued headlong in his selfishness until one day a deep sorrow fell on his heart. He came away from a church service realizing that he had thrown away one of the most precious gifts in his life—his family. But his life had become such a tangled web of lies and deceit that he could see no way back to the truth. In desperation, Sam called out to the God of mercy to do what only He could do.

Pastor Dale had the amazing privilege of watching God break through Sam and Gracie's marriage. The transformation was miraculous as love and closeness reentered their home and their marriage relationship was reconciled.

Over time, Sam and Gracie became leaders in the church, and now they help to bring a message of hope and healing to other broken and hurting marriages and homes.

———

Mark Henry, another member of my brother Dale's church, was a Christian, but he had been living a life away from the Lord for some time. He had turned to substance abuse and was addicted to drugs. He was miserable and became chronically depressed.

One day, Mark decided to take his own life. His father had recently died, which troubled Mark greatly. Mark took a gun and went to his father's grave, intent on killing himself at the place that was symbolic to him of all the pain in his life.

Mark raised the gun to his head, and right before he pulled the trigger, he heard the voice of God say, "You're just going to throw away your life anyway, why not throw it into My hands."

Mark prayed for the first time in years. As he prayed, the power of the Lord hit him. He fell on his father's grave, weeping and repenting of his sins. Instantly, he was healed of both his depression and his addiction.

That was 19 years ago. Mark now walks closely with the Lord and is a leader at church.

————————

Bernie Bovenkamp, head of the Starfish Ministries relief agency, was leading a missions trip to an orphanage in Haiti a few years ago. The village where the group was working is called Tricotte. It is so remote that it can't be found on any map. To get there, missionaries travel on paved roads that turn into dirt roads until they run out; then they have to travel for miles up the sides of a riverbank and finally ascend a winding goat path.

High up in the village of Tricotte, Bernie suddenly got very sick. He recognized the pain as kidney stones—he had experienced such an attack twice before, back in the States, and both times needed to be hospitalized. Kidney stones are not usually life-threatening, but the condition puts a person in a horrendous amount of pain. Bernie needed to be flown back to the States immediately. One problem: Driving out of Tricotte is never an easy task. There are no phones or cell phone reception to call for help. No ambulances or doctors for miles. The area is too steep to land an emergency helicopter. Bernie was stuck.

The pain had hit him at 2 A.M. Bernie lay in pain all that day. At 7 P.M., four of the older boys from the orphanage in Tricotte climbed up to the hut where Bernie was staying. They began to sing over him, and then quoted Scriptures, and then prayed—all in the Creole language, and all at once. As the four orphans cried out to God, Bernie said the clouds parted. One moment, he was in unspeakable pain. The next moment, the pain subsided in a flash. God broke through. Bernie got up the next morning and continued leading the trip as if he had never been in pain.

When Bernie tells that story today, he just smiles. It's one of many breakthrough stories he has witnessed firsthand through the years. One of the ways that he sees God break through each month is with the mission agency's finances. About two-thirds of the $32,000 monthly expenses needed to run the orphanages and schools under the Starfish umbrella are not guaranteed income—meaning that each month there is no assurance that more than $11,000 of that money will be there. But month after month, all the bills keep getting paid.

Once, a few months ago, Bernie was paying bills at the end of the month and was exactly $500 short—to the penny. This was the first time this had happened in the decade or so of running the ministry. He prayed, trusted, waited and fortunately was able to cover the shortness from another source.

About a week after paying bills, Bernie ran into a man while out doing errands. "Oh, I completely forgot," the man said. "I had a check in my pocket to give you a couple of weeks ago and it slipped my mind."

The man handed Bernie a check for $500.

These are just a few examples of a breakthrough God at work. Only God can bring hope in the midst of so many situations. These stories are mostly about times of instant change, but God will also often bring breakthroughs over a period of time. When we say to ourselves, *There's no way out,* those are the times when Christ says, "I can make a way of escape" (see 1 Cor. 10:13). God is our Maker. He knows how we were created better than anybody. Only God can bring perfect peace, fullness of joy, or make sense from a tragedy. When God breaks through, our brains may wonder what's going on, but our spirits will leap for joy.

What will a breakthrough look like in our lives? Each of us is different, and God works in us in different ways at different times. He doesn't promise an instant breakthrough for everybody, but He does promise His presence and His goodness. A breakthrough will look different for different people.

So run to Him. Trust in Him. Release your life to Him. He will satisfy the hunger of your soul like nothing else.

PRAYER

O Lord, I don't know exactly what a breakthrough
will look like in my life. I only know that You are
the breakthrough God. I resist the lies of the
enemy that tell me You are far away, uninterest-
ed, unable and unwilling to meet me here.
I stand up and declare that the light of Your
presence in me is stronger, deeper and brighter
than my darkest fear or impossible situation.
You are the God of the impossible, and nothing is
too difficult for You! I commit my life into Your
hands. You are good. You are wise. I trust in You.
Break through like only You can do. Amen.

CHAPTER 8

NEVER THE SAME AGAIN

It is God who arms me with strength
and makes my way perfect.

PSALM 18:32

My brother Dale told me about a time recently when he came home and joined his son, who was watching an L.A. Lakers basketball game on TV. Dale can get really worked up over sports, and this time was no exception. At one point, the Lakers fell behind, and Dale was simply beside himself—howling, pacing the room, holding his head in his hands.

Finally, his son could take no more.

"Dad," he said, "you need to know that this is a taped game. It was already played earlier today, and the Lakers already won. "

The Lakers had *already won.*

It took some time for Dale to adjust emotionally to the news, but from that moment on, everything changed for him. He got himself a bowl of popcorn, sat down in his chair, relaxed and faced the game with complete peace, joy and confidence.

That story describes our life as believers. We already know how our "game" will turn out. Because of the cross, Jesus Christ has triumphed in the battle over sin and death. He is the victor, and there is coming a day when all will be made right. On that day there will be no more crying, no more suffering, no more guilt, pain, sorrow or fear. *Jesus has already won.*

Knowing the outcome helps us keep life in perspective today. We may feel like we're 12 buckets down with 5 seconds left on the clock, but we can relax—we have Christ. We've already won the game. Yes, we still have battles, but we've won the war. A mind-set of victory can be ours today.

As this book draws to a close, let me say one last time that the way to stay within the framework of a victory mind-set—the way to have a breakthrough—is to seek a relationship with God Himself. At the end of the day, He is always the answer to what we're searching for, and He is enough.

Breakthrough comes not with the outer things that God can do for us but in the personhood of Christ Himself. To seek a breakthrough is not about seeking a changed life—not ultimately, anyway. It's about seeking the One who is able to bring change. Seek His face—that's the entire message of this book. Seek Him and worship Him. He has all the beauty. He has all the wholeness. He has all the strength and endurance. He's the One with perfect peace and joy. It is He who has all the fullness of life that we so desperately need. When we draw close to God, all His riches fill our lives. That's when change happens.

A BREAKTHROUGH GOD AND HIS BREAKTHROUGH PEOPLE

The God we serve wants us to have breakthroughs. His entire nature is about releasing us from bondage and darkness and breaking through to free us, give us light and increase our faith and joy.

Everything about Him—the Incarnation; how He developed His disciples; His ministry to the broken, the sick and the marginalized; His resurrection that defeated death once and for all—is about breakthrough. So let's not hesitate to ask Him for breakthrough.

Asking God for a breakthrough is like asking birds to fly or fish to swim—they were made to fly and swim; it's their very nature. The same is true of our Lord. Breakthrough is what He does because it's His very nature to bring breakthrough. He is the breakthrough God. So yes, what a blessing to know that the God we worship and seek will bring to us all His treasure chest of gifts and blessings.

Because our God's very nature is to bring us breakthrough, we are called to be breakthrough people, too. Our lives are characterized by breakthrough because of our close relationship with Him.

We are not called to be Copers—just biding our time in this life until we die. We are called to be Catalysts—people who actively position ourselves for a breakthrough. We all have barriers to our relationship with the Lord, but we can't let the blockers stop us. God is big enough, strong enough, loving enough, wise enough and caring enough to break through to our lives, no matter who we are or what we've done. So don't put it off. Pray for a breakthrough now; pray for a breakthrough today. Pray that the blockers in your life will no longer hinder your closeness to the Lord.

What are some specific prayers you can pray to become a breakthrough person?

Pray that God would break your heart over the needs of people. As you become a breakthrough person, you can't stand the thought of people trapped in sorrow with no knowledge or access to their breakthrough God. When you become a breakthrough person, you seek these people out; you go to them, find them, become their friend and care for them.

Pray that God would call you to whatever task He has for you and then give you the strength and grace to finish that work. In prayer, we are able to give up our rights to an easy, comfortable, predictable life. Our one passion becomes living our lives for the Lord.

Pray for the strength to live every day to make a difference, to do whatever you can to cause light to shine into darkness. These are the prayers of Catalysts—not simply that the Lord would help us through each day, but that God would use us to encounter people in specific ways, and that we would become the vessels He uses to answer those prayers.

Pray that God would enable you to live by faith and not by fear. We were created to experience a life that is marked by breakthrough. We were created for freedom and not bondage, for joy and not suffering, for peace and not trouble. And we don't just want one breakthrough; we want a breakthrough lifestyle—

we want a breakthrough today and every day.

WELCOME TO THE BEGINNING

I've been in some amazing worship gatherings. Do you know what I'm talking about? It just feels like you can't jump any higher, cry any harder, bow any further or sing any louder. But at times you can walk away from that and think, *Now what?*

It's easy to feel that way at the end of a book too. *Well, that was inspiring, but now what?*

The answer is straightforward: One last breakthrough releaser comes when we invite someone else to the party. When we pray for breakthrough, our prayers are not limited to ourselves. One of the reasons we experience breakthrough is to give it away—we are to pray for breakthroughs for other people.

A pastor told me that his brother-in-law had recently died a tragic death. They were in a prayer meeting singing the song "Break Through," and he was suddenly impressed to turn the song into a prayer for his mother-in-law who had just lost her son. So he told the group, "Let's sing the song again, but this time pray it over someone you know who is in need." The pastor said that a renewed sense of the

Spirit came over the place. Not only were powerful prayers offered up, but breakthrough also came anew for those who were interceding for others! It's like when God keeps giving—our hands get full and we can't hold on to it all, so we just have to keep giving it away. We give out of abundance.

So I want to ask you to do something: Read chapter 1 again. And this time, read it through with others in mind. Invite them to know the breakthrough God who is at work in their hearts today.

CLOSING THOUGHT

The end truly is the beginning. In the last book of the Bible, after all the battles of the Old Testament and the miracles of the New, Jesus says this:

> Here I am! I stand at the door and knock. If anyone hears my voice and opens the door, I will come in and eat with him, and he with me (Rev. 3:20).

I believe this is your invitation right now, this very moment. I believe that Jesus is saying to you and to me,

Can you hear Me? Do you want Me? I'm closer than you think. Your breakthrough is here. Your breakthrough is Me. I'm knocking on your heart's door. When you open your heart—and I mean open the most tender places of your heart—you will discover that I am your Redeemer, your Rebuilder, your Restorer and Healer. I am the breakthrough God! Did you hear Me? *I am the breakthrough God!* Open the door and bow before Me. Worship Me, and I will come in. I will touch you in the deepest part of your heart where no one else can go—and when I do, you will never be the same again.

PRAYER

Break through, break through all my doubts
Break through, break through all my fears
Break through, that I may worship You.
Break through, break through all my pain
Break through, all my guilt and my shame
Break through, like only You can do.

You are brighter than my darkest night
Stronger than my toughest fight

Just one touch from You my King, my Friend
And I'll never be the same again.[1]

Note
1. Tommy Walker, "Break Through," © 2005.

Also Available in the Best-Selling Worship Series

The Unquenchable Worshipper
Coming Back to the Heart of Worship
Matt Redman
ISBN 08307.29135

The Heart of Worship Files
Featuring Contributions from Some
of Today's Most Experienced
Lead Worshippers
Matt Redman, General Editor
ISBN 08307.32616

Here I Am to Worship
Never Lose the Wonder
of Worshiping the Savior
Tim Hughes
ISBN 08307.33221

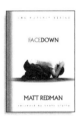

Facedown
When You Face Up to God's Glory, You
Find Yourself Facedown in Worship
Matt Redman
ISBN 08307.32462

Also Available in the Best-Selling Worship Series

Inside, Out Worship
Insights for Passionate and
Purposeful Worship
Matt Redman and Friends
ISBN 08307.37103

For the Audience of One
Worshiping the One and Only
in Everything You Do
Mike Pilavachi
ISBN 08307.37049

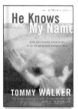

He Knows My Name
How God Knows Each of Us in
an Unspeakably Intimate Way
Tommy Walker
ISBN 08307.36360

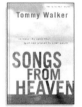

Songs from Heaven
Release the Song That God
Has Placed in Your Heart
Tommy Walker
ISBN 08307.37839

Pick Up a Copy at Your Favorite Christian Bookstore!

Visit **www.regalbooks.com** to join **Regal's FREE e-newsletter.**
You'll get useful **excerpts from our newest releases** and **special
access to online chats with your favorite authors.** Sign up today!

Regal
God's Word for Your World™
www.regalbooks.com

Also Available in the Best-Selling Worship Series

The Worship God Is Seeking
An Exploration of Worship and the Kingdom of God
David Ruis
ISBN 08307.36921

Blessed be Your Name
Worshipping God on the Road Marked With Suffering
Matt & Beth Redman
ISBN 08307.38193

Breakthrough
How to Experience God's Presence When You Need It Most
Tommy Walker
ISBN 08307.39149

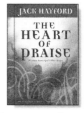

The Justice God Is Seeking
Responding to the Heart of God Through Compassionate Worship
David Ruis
ISBN 08307.41976

The Heart of Praise
Worship After God's Own Heart
Jack Hayford
ISBN 08307.37855